God
of the Possible

*A Biblical Introduction
to the Open View of God*

Gregory A. Boyd

Baker Books

A Division of Baker Book House Co
Grand Rapids, Michigan 49516

© 2000 by Gregory A. Boyd

Published by Baker Books
a division of Baker Book House Company
P.O. Box 6287, Grand Rapids, MI 49516-6287

Printed in the United States of America

ISBN 0-8010-6290-X

Library of Congress Cataloging-in-Publication Data is on file at the Library of Congress, Washington, D.C.

Unless otherwise indicated, Scripture quotations are from the New Revised Standard Version of the Bible, copyright 1989 by the Division of Christian Education of the National Council of the Churches of Christ in the USA. Used by permission.

Scripture quotations identified KJV are from the King James Version of the Bible.

Scripture quotations identified NASB are from the NEW AMERICAN STANDARD BIBLE ®. Copyright © The Lockman Foundation 1960, 1962, 1963, 1968, 1971, 1972, 1973, 1975, 1977, 1995. Used by permission.

Scripture quotations identified NIV are from the HOLY BIBLE, NEW INTERNATIONAL VERSION®. NIV®. Copyright © 1973, 1978, 1984 by International Bible Society. Used by permission of Zondervan Publishing House. All rights reserved.

For further information about Dr. Greg Boyd's ministry, publications, and theology, visit his web site:

http://www.gregboyd.org

For current information about all releases from Baker Book House, visit our web site:
http://www.bakerbooks.com

This book is dedicated to Tyler and Chelsea DeArmond.

I enjoy your friendship.
I appreciate your assistance.
I admire your brilliance.
I applaud your discipleship.

Contents

Preface

One evening about seventeen years ago, I came upon 2 Kings 20 while reading my Bible. I read that King Hezekiah was sick and the Lord told him through the prophet Isaiah, "Thus says the LORD: Set your house in order, for you shall die; you shall not recover" (v. 1). Hezekiah then prayed earnestly and persuaded the Lord to add fifteen years to his life (v. 6).

I'd read these verses many times before, but for some reason they struck me as more profound and more peculiar this particular evening. What puzzled me was this: Was God being sincere when he had Isaiah tell Hezekiah he wouldn't recover from his illness? And if so, then must we not believe that God really changed his mind when he decided to add fifteen years to Hezekiah's life?

I began to wonder how this could be true if God foreknew all that was going to happen ahead of time, as I had been taught to believe all my Christian life. How could God have truly *changed his mind* in response to a prayer if the prayer he was responding to was forever in his mind? How could Scripture say God added fifteen years to Hezekiah's life if it was certain to God that Hezekiah was going to live those "extra" fifteen years all along?

These questions initiated a course of study that lasted several years. I wanted to resolve for myself whether or not the Bible taught that God always knows what is going to happen an eternity before it happens. In the course of this prolonged study, I combed through the entire Bible. I carefully noted every passage that seemed to support the view that the future is exhaustively settled in the mind of God as well as every passage, such as 2 Kings 20, that seemed to suggest the future is to some extent open and that God does not know every detail about what will come to pass. I then pondered various ways the two sets of passages might be reconciled into a coherent theological perspective.

About three years later, I became convinced that the customary view—that the future is exhaustively settled and that God knows it as such—was mistaken. I came to believe that the future is, to some degree at least, open-ended and that God knows it as such. I began to embrace what is now generally called the "open view" of God. Next to the central doctrines of the Christian faith, the issue of whether the future is exhaustively settled or partially open is relatively unimportant. It certainly is not a doctrine Christians should ever divide over. Still, I have to confess that the perspective I came to embrace has had a rather profound impact on my life.

Among other things, I have found that parts of the Bible and certain aspects of life make much better sense to me now than they did before. I have discovered a new appreciation and excitement regarding my own responsibility in bringing about the future. The passion and urgency with which I pray has increased immensely. And, in part because of this position, I no longer struggle with the problem of evil the way I used to. (These matters are discussed in chapter 3.)

In this book I'd like to share the fruit of my investigation. I will explain how a Bible-believing Christian could come to believe, on the authority of God's Word, that the future is not exhaustively settled. I will explain the philo-

sophical basis and defense of this open view and flesh out
how this view could have positive ramifications in a person's life.

I do not know whether you, the reader, will come to share
my convictions. But I believe that if you consider carefully
the case set forth in this book, it will illuminate aspects of
God's Word that you may not have noticed before. It will
open your mind to an intriguing—and in my estimation,
wonderful—way of thinking about God and the future.

I must express a profound word of love and appreciation
to my adorable wife of twenty years, Shelley Boyd. Thank
you for tolerating, even embracing, my manic character
when I get a project like this under my skin. I am very grate-
ful to Chelsea DeArmond, whose amazing editorial skills
helped make this work readable for laypeople. Thanks also
to my brilliant assistant, Tyler DeArmond, as well as to my
professorial colleagues, Paul Eddy, David Clark, and Jim
Bilbey. You have provided me with much-needed critical
feedback, and this book is the better for it.

Finally, my deep appreciation and admiration must be
expressed to Jay Barnes, provost of Bethel College, and
Truett Lawson, executive pastor of the Minnesota Baptist
Conference. Your irenic leadership throughout the controversy over this issue that has engulfed our denomination
the last three years has been exemplary. With each of you
I pray that our Baptist fellowship, and evangelicalism in
general, will come to see more clearly that the love with
which believers debate issues is more important to God
than the sides we take.

To all, I offer this humble perspective for your consideration in love.

Introduction

Most evangelical Christians take it for granted that God knows everything that is ever going to take place. They have been taught that the future is completely settled in God's mind and has been so from all eternity. This view is sometimes called the "classical view of divine foreknowledge." Though it has always been the majority view in the church, it is the view I will be arguing *against* throughout this work.

If you think about the matter deeply, the classical view raises a number of thorny questions. For example, if every choice you've ever made was certain an eternity before you made it, were you really free when you made each choice? Could you have chosen differently if it was eternally certain you'd make the choice you did?

Even more troubling, if God foreknew that Adolf Hitler would send six million Jews to their death, why did he go ahead and create a man like that? If I unleash a mad dog I am certain will bite you, am I not responsible for my dog's behavior? If so, how is God not responsible for the behavior of evil people he "unleashes" on the world—if, in fact, he is absolutely certain of what they will do once "unleashed"?

Moreover, if God is eternally certain that various individuals will end up being eternally damned, why does he go ahead and create them? If hell is worse than never being born, as Jesus suggests (Matt. 26:24), wouldn't an all-loving God refrain from creating people he is certain will end up there? If God truly doesn't want "any to perish"(2 Peter 3:9), why does he create people he is certain will do just that?[1]

Indeed, if the destiny of every person who will eventually end up in hell is settled before they are born, why does God continue to try to get them to accept his grace throughout their lives—as though there were genuine hope for them? Would *you* spend a lifetime trying to accomplish something you were certain could never be accomplished?

The most serious questions about the classical view of foreknowledge, however, relate to the Bible. If the future is indeed exhaustively settled in God's mind, as the classical view holds, why does the Bible repeatedly describe God changing his mind? Why does the Bible say that God frequently alters his plans, cancels prophecies in the light of changing circumstances, and speaks about the future as a "maybe," a "perhaps," or a "possibility"? Why does it describe God as expressing uncertainty about the future, being disappointed in the way things turn out, and even occasionally regretting the outcome of his own decisions? If the Bible is always true—and I, for one, assume that it is—how can we reconcile this way of talking about God (to be discussed in chapter 2) with the notion that the future is exhaustively settled in his mind?

Questions such as these led me to a biblical and theological investigation of God's foreknowledge seventeen years ago. To my surprise, I came to the conclusion that something was amiss in the classical understanding of divine foreknowledge. I came to believe that the future was, indeed, *partly* determined and foreknown by God, but also partly *open* and known by God as such. In short, I embraced what has come to be labeled the "open view" of God.

In this book I want to share with the reader the biblical evidence that led me to this conclusion as well as some of the theological and practical considerations that I believe support it. Before doing so, however, a few introductory comments about the timing and nature of this book will help set the stage for what is to follow.

The Reason for This Book

I am putting the fruit of my investigation into writing at the present time for two reasons. First, when I initially embraced the open view of God, there was little controversy surrounding it. I knew it was not the traditional view, but neither I nor those who shared it considered it anything like heresy. How quickly things change! Today the controversy over the open view of God is one of the hottest topics within evangelical circles, and, unfortunately, some people are beginning to toss around the alarmist label "heresy."

What is particularly sad about the current state of this debate is that Scripture seems to be playing a small role in it. Most of the published criticisms raised against the open view have largely ignored the biblical grounds on which open theists base their position. For example, in his recent book, *God the Father Almighty,* Millard Erickson devotes an entire chapter to refuting the open view, but he never once interacts with any of the biblical arguments that support the open theist position. Unfortunately, this is typical of literature that critiques the open view. The open view is consistently portrayed as though it was driven by unbiblical and invalid philosophical arguments. While I happen to believe that the open view is the most philosophically compelling view available (see chapter 4), the primary consideration that motivates me and most other open theists to embrace it is not philosophy but Scripture. I feel it is time to establish the biblical case in as clear, thorough, and concise a manner as possible.

Second, most of the debate surrounding the open view of God has been quite technical and restricted to sophisticated philosophical and theological journals and books. While I consider such discussions to be valuable, I also believe this issue is too important and too practically significant to be limited to academic circles. By the time the various issues trickle down from the ivory academic towers to the masses, much of the information has been lost or distorted. I believe there is currently a need to present this issue in a manner that can include as many laypeople as possible. This book attempts to do just that.

I am aware that some of the important nuances and arguments on both sides of the debate will have to be discarded to accomplish this. I am also aware that some of my professional colleagues may, with some justification, accuse me of oversimplification. If this book informs and motivates the audience it is intended for, however, I will most happily stand by my decision.

The Method of My Investigation

As we will discover in chapters 1 and 2, there are two categories of passages in the Bible that apply to the topic of God's foreknowledge and the nature of the future. Most of us are familiar with the many passages that depict God as foreknowing and/or predestining certain things about the future. For reasons to be made clear in the next chapter, I label this group of passages the "motif of future determinism." What is not so often appreciated, however, is that there is another major motif that runs throughout Scripture. I label this the "motif of future openness." This motif is seen in many passages of Scripture that depict God as facing a partly open future. He does not control and/or foreknow exactly what is going to happen.

The classical view of divine foreknowledge interprets the first motif as speaking about God *as he truly is* and the second motif as speaking about God only as he *appears to be* or as *figures of speech*. In other words, whenever the Bible suggests that God knows and/or controls the future, this is taken literally. Whenever it suggests that God knows the future in terms of possibilities, however, this is not taken literally.[2]

My approach to these two motifs differs from this. I do not assume that the motif of future openness is less literal than the motif of future determinism. Nothing in the biblical texts that constitute the motif of future openness suggests they are less literal than the texts that constitute the motif of future determinism. As far as I can discern, there are two reasons why classical theologians conclude that the second motif must not be literal—neither has to do with the biblical evidence.

First, classical theologians don't see how they can reconcile the motif of future openness with the first motif of future determinism if the first motif is interpreted literally. Second, classical theologians believe on philosophical grounds that the motif of future openness is "beneath" God if it is taken literally. In their view, it demeans God's sovereignty to suggest that he does not foreknow everything that will ever take place. Hence, verses that suggest this must be interpreted as either speaking in terms of appearance or as figures of speech.

As I hope to show in chapter 1, there is no difficulty in reconciling the two motifs so long as one doesn't assume at the start that the motif of future determinism tells the whole story about God's foreknowledge. If we don't assume that the future is entirely settled, there is an easy way to integrate the motif of future determinism with the motif of future openness. As I hope to show in chapter 2, far from being "beneath" God, Scripture describes the openness of God to the future as one of his attributes of greatness. I will argue that a God who knows all possibilities, experiences novelty, and is willing to engage in an appropriate element of risk is more exalted than a God who faces an eternally settled future.

In any event, the distinctive aspect of my approach is that I regard both motifs to be equally descriptive of the way God and the future actually are. On this basis, I arrive at the conclusion that the future is to some degree *settled* and known by God as such, and to some degree *open* and known by God as such. To some extent, God knows the future as *definitely* this way and *definitely* not that way. To some extent, however, he knows it as *possibly* this way and *possibly* not that way.

This is the "open view of God" or, as I prefer, the "open view of the future." It does not hold that the future is wide open. Much of it, open theists concede, is settled ahead of time, either by God's predestining will or by existing earthly causes, but it is not *exhaustively* settled ahead of time. To whatever degree the future is yet open to be decided by free agents, it is unsettled. To this extent, God knows it as a realm of possibilities, not certainties.

The Real Issue Addressed in This Book

The careful reader may have already discerned a subtle but very important point regarding this debate about God's foreknowledge—namely, it is not really about God's knowledge at all. It is rather a debate about the nature of the future. Though open theists are often accused of denying God's omniscience because they deny the classical view of

16

foreknowledge, this criticism is unfounded. Open theists affirm God's omniscience as emphatically as anybody does. The issue is not whether God's knowledge is perfect. It is. The issue is about the nature of the reality that God perfectly knows. More specifically, what is the content of the reality of the future? Whatever it is, we all agree that God perfectly knows it.

The classical view answers this question by saying that the content of the future consists exclusively of things that are settled. The "definiteness" of every event—the fact that it will occur *this* way and not any other way—eternally precedes the actual occurrence of the event, so God eternally foreknows every event in a definite manner. In other words, the future contains no possibilities—things that may be this way or may be that way. It looks this way to us only because we are limited in our knowledge.

Open theists, by contrast, hold that the future consists partly of settled realities and partly of unsettled realities. Some things about the future are *possibly* this way and *possibly* that way. Hence, precisely because they also hold that God knows all of reality perfectly, open theists believe that God knows the future as consisting of both unsettled possibilities and settled certainties. In this sense, open theists could (and should) affirm that God knows the future perfectly. It's just that they understand the future *as it is now* to include genuine possibilities.[3]

If God does not foreknow future free actions, it is not because his knowledge of the future is in any sense incomplete. It's because there is, in this view, *nothing definite there for God to know!* His lack of definite foreknowledge of future free actions limits him no more than does the fact that, say, he does not know that there is a monkey sitting next to me right now. As a matter of fact, there is no monkey sitting next to me, so it's hardly ascribing ignorance to God to insist that he doesn't know one is there. In just the same way, one is not ascribing ignorance to God by insisting that he doesn't foreknow future free actions if indeed free actions do not exist to be known until free agents create them.

A person may choose to affirm that there is a monkey next to me or that the settledness of future free actions exists before agents choose them. So they may choose to affirm that God knows there is a monkey next to me and that he foreknows future free actions as settled, but in doing so, they are disagreeing about the content of reality, not about the omniscience of God. They shouldn't accuse a person who denies there is a monkey next to me (or that future free actions are settled ahead of time) of denying God's omniscience simply because we disagree about the content of reality.

It's important to keep this distinction in mind throughout this book. Those who oppose the open view of God on the grounds that it compromises God's omniscience are simply misguided. The debate between the open and classical understandings of divine foreknowledge is completely a debate over the nature of the future: Is it exhaustively settled from all eternity, or is it partly open? *That* is the question at hand, nothing else.

The Title

The title of this book, *God of the Possible,* is directly related to this last point. My fundamental thesis is that the classical theological tradition became misguided when, under the influence of Hellenistic philosophy, it defined God's perfection in static, timeless terms. All change was considered an imperfection and thus not applicable to God.[4] Given this definition of divine perfection, there was no way to conceive of God as entertaining real possibilities. In the classical view, God never genuinely faces a "maybe," a "perhaps," or a "possibly this way or possibly that way." For God, reality is eternally definite, settled, fixed, and certain. Since God knows reality perfectly, it followed for classical theology that reality must be eternally and exhaustively settled. Humans experience the future as possibly one way and possibly another only because we are imperfect.

This view is misguided on biblical, theological, and practical grounds. Biblically, God is repeatedly depicted as facing a partially open future. Theologically, several unsolvable problems inherent in the classical view can be avoided when one accepts that God is the God of the possible and not simply a God of eternally static certainties. Practically, a God of eternally static certainties is incapable of interacting with humans in a relevant way. The God of the possible, by contrast, is a God who can work with us to truly change what *might* have been into what *should* be.

The Outline

The outline of this book is as follows. In the first chapter I will lay out and critique the "motif of future determinism," which forms the basis of the classical view of divine foreknowledge. My goal in this chapter is to show that while this motif warrants the conclusion that God controls and/or foreknows *much* of what is to come, it does not warrant the conclusion that God controls and/or foreknows *all* that is to come. There is, therefore, room for us to take the motif of future openness literally and conclude that some of the future is open, for it is not controlled and/or foreknown by God as settled.

Chapter 2 discusses this second scriptural motif. The goal of this chapter is to explicate several passages that depict the future as partially open and that God therefore knows it as such. I will attempt to demonstrate that it is very difficult to view these passages as depicting God only as he appears or as nonliteral figures of speech. There are no good exegetical or theological grounds for interpreting the motif of future openness any differently than we interpret the motif of future determinism.

In chapter 3, I move from theory to application. This chapter answers the question, What difference does any of this make in my life? I discuss some practical areas in which I think the open view can make a positive difference.

In the concluding chapter, I address the most frequently asked questions and the most frequently raised objections against the open view. If a theological position is true, it ought to be able to handle any and all objections and questions raised against it—at least better than competing positions. Some readers might want to regard portions of this chapter as "optional." Though I attempted to keep this material on a level that is readable for nonspecialists, some of the topics are philosophical and may be challenging for some and simply uninteresting for others.

Our Attitude in Discussing Controversial Issues

Finally, it's vitally important that we keep this issue and the multitude of other issues that Christians debate in perspective. Jesus' final prayer to the Father for his church was that "they may be one, as we are one" (John 17:22). Believers are called to exhibit a loving unity among each other that reflects nothing less than the eternal, perfect love of the Trinity!

This does not mean that we must always agree on all things, any more than the love between a husband and wife means that they must always agree. It does mean, however, that we must agree to love one another amidst our disagreements. If we only love those who agree with us, we are in fact not loving others at all; we are only loving the (assumed) "rightness" of our own ideas! Disagreeing with one another need not, and should not, be scary and divisive, so long as we keep our hearts and minds focused on the person of Jesus Christ. Indeed, when our hearts and minds are properly focused, our dialogues with one another, however impassioned they may be, become the means by which we lovingly help each other appreciate aspects of God's Word we might otherwise overlook or fail to understand.

Yes, the debate about the nature of the future is an important issue. For lovers of truth, all theological issues are important. But compared to our common faith in the person of Jesus Christ and the importance of our loving unity in him, this issue and most other theological issues are peripheral. Again, this doesn't mean that we should pretend that our differences don't exist, as one might expect from a dysfunctional family. The opposite is true. It means that we must face our differences and discuss them openly in love (Eph. 4:15). This is how we teach each other and grow together in truth and love.

Though I will not conceal the depth of my conviction as I write, the reader should always remember that it is with this attitude that I am sharing the results of my investigation on this topic. And I pray it is with this attitude that the reader carefully and critically considers the fruit of my labor.

ONE

The Classical View
of Divine Foreknowledge

As mentioned in the introduction, two motifs in Scripture pertain to the nature of the future and thus to the content of God's foreknowledge. The first expresses and celebrates God's sovereign control and foreknowledge of the future. The second expresses and celebrates an open aspect of the future and God's willingness to adapt to it. The classical view of divine foreknowledge is founded on the conviction that only the first motif describes God *as he really is*. The second motif is considered nonliteral in this view. In contrast, the open view is founded on the conviction that *both* motifs describe God as he really is.

In this chapter, I present an overview of the first motif and critique its application in the classical view of foreknowledge. In the next chapter, I present an overview of the second motif and show why open theists believe it requires the rejection of the classical view of foreknowledge.

Foreknowledge and Classical Theism

The Unchanging God

Before discussing the motif of future determinism in Scripture, it may prove helpful to place the classical view of divine foreknowledge in a broader theological context. The classical view of divine foreknowledge comes from what is generally called "the classical view of God." Most theologians since the time of Augustine (fourth to fifth century) have espoused this view in one form or another.

According to classical theology, God is unchanging *in every respect*. Not only his character, but also his will, his knowledge, and his experience never vary. They are what they are from all eternity. If this is so, then of course God's knowledge of the future must be unchanging. It can never come into being, nor can it ever be adjusted. It is eternally the same. It is forever settled as a "this" and "not that." There can be no "maybe" in God's knowledge, a "possibly this" or a "possibly that." Hence, whatever takes place in history, from events of great significance to the buzzing of a particular fly, must take place exactly as God eternally foreknew it would take place. The future is exhaustively settled and eternally known by God as such.

Two Versions of the Classical Understanding of Foreknowledge

Classical theologians do not agree on *how* the future is eternally settled, however. Some follow Augustine and

Calvin and maintain that the future will be a certain way *because God foreknows* it this way. Others follow Arminius and argue that God foreknows the future a certain way *because the future simply will be that way*. In other words, classical theologians disagree about what comes first. Does God's foreknowledge determine the future, or does the future determine God's foreknowledge?

Many followers of Augustine and Calvin maintain that since God alone exists eternally, the eternal settledness of the future could only come from him. Followers of Arminius usually admit that the cause of God's eternal foreknowledge is a mystery, but insist that unless we accept this mystery we cannot avoid the dreadful conclusion that God is ultimately responsible for everything that transpires in history, including evil.

In any event, both schools of thought agree that the future is eternally settled and that God eternally knows it as such. This constitutes the heart of the classical view of divine foreknowledge as well as the crucial point that separates the classical view from the open view.

A Third Option

Open theists agree with some followers of Augustine and Calvin that future events cannot cause God to know them. We agree that if God foreknows a future event, it must either be because he determined it or because it is an inevitable effect of past or present causes. However, we also agree with the followers of Arminius that if *all* future events are determined by God, then he must be ultimately responsible for everything about the future, including evil. Where we disagree with both views is that we deny that Scripture teaches that the future is *exhaustively* settled. We hold that God determines (and thus foreknows as settled) *some,* but not *all,* of the future.

For all who believe in the infallible authority of Scripture, the issue must be settled by a comprehensive investigation of God's Word. While some (including myself) argue that the development of the classical view of God was decisively influenced by pagan philosophy, classical theologians have always maintained that it is deeply rooted in Scripture. This chapter will investigate this claim as it pertains to the classical view of foreknowledge.

Since it is important to fully understand and appreciate the strengths of a position before we critique it, our first objective will be to examine those passages that most strongly support the classical position. Following this, I will reexamine this material, asking whether it actually proves that the future is exhaustively settled.

As mentioned earlier, I am not yet attempting to prove that Scripture actually exhibits a partly open view of the future—that is the task of the next chapter. For now, I am simply attempting to show that the biblical material used to support the view that the future is exhaustively settled doesn't, in fact, prove this point. I will argue that it only proves that *some* of the future is settled. If so, there is room beside the motif of future determinism to incorporate the motif of future openness, which will be examined in the next chapter.

The Biblical Foundation of the Classical Position

The Sovereign Lord of History

Undoubtedly the strongest statements in all of Scripture regarding the foreknowledge of God come from Isaiah. Here the Lord repeatedly demonstrates that he is the Lord of history and distinct from the idols many Jews were tempted to follow by showing that he can do what none of them can do—namely, declare the future. Hence, in Isaiah 46:9–10, the Lord declares:

> I am God, and there is no other;
> I am God, and there is no one like me,
> declaring the end from the beginning
> and from ancient times things not yet done.

Even more emphatic is Isaiah 48:3–5:

> The former things I declared long ago,
> they went out from my mouth and I made them
> known;
> then suddenly I did them and they came to pass.
> Because I know that you are obstinate,
> and your neck is an iron sinew
> and your forehead brass,
> I declared them to you from long ago,
> before they came to pass I announced them to you,
> so that you would not say, "My idol did them,
> my carved image and my cast image commanded
> them."

Defenders of the classical view of foreknowledge argue that these verses show that God is certain of all that is to come. They argue that if God can declare "the end from the beginning," what could possibly be uncertain to him?

Examples of God predicting future events throughout Scripture are interpreted as confirmations of the classical view of God's foreknowledge. For our present purposes, these can be broken down into five categories.

Foreknowledge of the Chosen People

First, God exhibits a remarkable knowledge about the future of his chosen people. For example, the Lord told Abraham that his offspring would be slaves in Egypt "for four hundred years," but afterward would "come out with great possessions" (Gen. 15:13–14). Similarly, when Israel was in captivity, the Lord promised them that after seventy years, "I will fulfill to you my promise and bring you back to this place [Jerusalem]. For surely I know the plans I have for you . . . plans for your welfare and not for harm, to give you a future with hope" (Jer. 29:10–11).

Foreknowledge of Individuals

Second, a number of times the Lord demonstrates foreknowledge of particular individuals and various events in their lives. Twice in Scripture the Lord names individuals before they are born and provides some detail about their lives. Josiah was to tear down the pagan altars and destroy the pagan priesthood that plagued Israel (1 Kings 13:2–3; see 2 Kings 22:1; 23:15–16), while Cyrus was to help rebuild Jerusalem (Isa. 44:28).

In a similar fashion, Jesus tells Peter ahead of time that he would deny him three times before the next morning (Matt. 26:34). Jesus also foretells Judas's betrayal of him (John 6:64, 70–71; 13:18–19; 17:12) and the fact that Peter would die a martyr's death (John 21:18–19). Just as impressively, David suggests that the exact length of his life was known by God before he was born. "In your book were written all the days that were formed for me," he writes, "when none of them as yet existed" (Ps. 139:16). Similarly, the Lord appointed Jeremiah to be "a prophet to the nations" when he was still in the womb (Jer. 1:5) and set Paul apart before he was born (Gal. 1:15–16). Defenders of the classical view of foreknowledge consider this evidence that God foreknows everything that every individual will do before he or she is born.

Finally, under this category, we should mention that a number of times the Lord prophesies that certain things were going to happen to various nations or cities. Often these prophecies involved the activity of particular individuals. For example, God foretells the succession of four kingdoms through Nebuchadnezzar's dream (Dan. 2:31–45). Most impressively, the Lord prophesies a number of details about the fate of Tyre (Ezek. 26:7–21). The fulfillment of this prophecy involved to a great extent the activity of one ruler, Alexander the Great, centuries after it was given. To defenders of the classical view of foreknowledge, this implies that God foreknew exactly what Alexander would choose to do centuries before he did it. And if this much can be foreknown as settled by God, they conclude, we have no reason to deny that *every* detail about the future is settled in God's mind.

Foreknowledge of Christ's Ministry

Third, many passages of Scripture make it clear that God foreknew and foreordained aspects of Christ's ministry, especially his death. Indeed, Scripture tells us that "[Christ] was destined before the foundation of the world" (1 Peter 1:20). The Old Testament contains many passages that anticipate his coming. For example, in Zechariah the Lord says that the Jews would someday "look on the one whom they have pierced [and] . . . mourn for him" (12:10), an apparent reference to Christ's crucifixion—centuries before crucifixion had been invented as a form of execution. Similarly, in Isaiah we read that the suffering servant would die "with the wicked" though he would be buried "with the rich" (53:9). Jesus, of course, was crucified as a common criminal but was buried in the tomb of the wealthy Joseph of Arimathea (Matt. 27:57–60).

Jesus also foretold what would happen to him several times throughout his own ministry. He would suffer "at the hands of the elders and chief priests and scribes, and be killed, and on the third day be raised" (Matt. 16:21; see also 20:17–19). When this actually happened, Scripture says it was "according to the definite plan and foreknowledge of God" (Acts 2:23; 4:28). Defenders of the classical view take this as confirmation that all of the future is foreknown by God as settled.

Foreknowledge of the Elect

Fourth, defenders of the classical view of foreknowledge argue that Scripture demonstrates that God foreknows, if not predestines, who his "elect" will be. Paul teaches us that "those whom [God] foreknew he also predestined to be conformed to the image of his Son" (Rom. 8:29). In Ephesians, he tells believers that "[God] chose us in Christ before the foundation of the world to be holy and blameless before him in love" (1:4). We were given grace "in Christ Jesus before the ages began" (2 Tim. 1:9). Defenders of the classical view argue that if we were "chosen" and "given grace" before the world began, God must have foreknown (if not foreordained) that we would believe before the world began as well.

Foreknowledge of End Times

The final category of passages that are relevant to the issue of God's foreknowledge are prophecies about the end times. In several instances, scriptural authors seem to make predictions about things that will take place at the end of history.

For example, Paul says that ". . . in later times some will renounce the faith by paying attention to deceitful spirits and teachings of demons" (1 Tim. 4:1). Among other things, these people "forbid marriage and demand abstinence from foods" (1 Tim. 4:3). He also informs his readers at Thessalonica that before the final day, a great "rebellion" would come and a certain "lawless one" would "[exalt] himself above every so-called god or object of worship" and would "[take] his seat in the temple of God, declaring himself to be God" (2 Thess. 2:3–4).

Finally, we should mention the Book of Revelation, since in the mind of many contemporary readers this book is about events that will occur at the very end of history. Some defenders of classical foreknowledge consider this further confirmation of the exhaustive settledness of the future.

A Reexamination of the Case for the Classical View

At first glance, the case for the classical view of divine foreknowledge seems impressive. Indeed, the reader at this point may be wondering how any believer in their right mind could deny it. I understand the sentiment—I was once there myself—but I encourage you to keep an open mind until all the evidence is in. Whenever we are used to hearing only one side of a story, it is easy to read our beliefs *into* the evidence rather than allowing all the evidence to speak for itself. If we truly want to hold beliefs that are determined by the Word of God and not simply by what we're used to believing, we must take care to examine *all* of Scripture and to consider objectively perspectives that may differ from the one we're used to.

In the remainder of this chapter, I will offer the reader explanations of the verses we just examined from a different perspective—the open perspective. I will show that while they celebrate God's sovereign control over the future, they do not teach that the future is *exhaustively* settled.

Declaring His Intentions

Isaiah 46

Let's begin with the most explicit and compelling verses in the Bible pertaining to God's foreknowledge: Isaiah 46 and 48. As we saw, Isaiah 46:9–10 tells us that God "[declares] the end from the beginning and from ancient times things not yet done." Does this imply that everything about the future is settled in God's mind? When the verse is read in context, I believe the answer is no.

Immediately after telling us that he declares "from ancient times things not yet done," the Lord adds, "*My purpose* shall stand, and *I will fulfill* my intention" (Isa. 46:10b). The Lord is not appealing to information about the future he happens to possess; instead, he is appealing to *his own intentions* about the future. He foreknows that certain things are going to take place because he knows *his own purpose and intention* to bring these events about. As sovereign Lord of history, he has decided to settle *this much* about the future.

The point is even more emphatic in the next sentence: "*I* have spoken, and *I* will bring it to pass; *I* have planned, and *I* will do it" (Isa. 46:11). The Lord's announcement that he declares "the end from the beginning" must be understood in the light of this specification. He tells us that he is talking about *his own* will and *his own* plans. He declares that the future is settled to the extent that he is going to determine it, but nothing in the text requires that we believe that *everything* that will ever come to pass will do so according to his will and thus is settled ahead of time. Indeed, if everything came to pass according to his will, one wonders why God has to try to overcome the obstinacy of the Israelites with these assertions about particular future intentions. Wouldn't the Israelites' obstinancy itself be controlled by God?

Isaiah 48

The same holds true for Isaiah 48:3–5. The Lord says, "The former things I declared long ago . . . then suddenly

I did them." The Lord did this because he did not want the
Israelites saying, "My idol did them" (48:5). In other words,
as a supernatural means of confronting the lie that idols
have power to bring about events, Yahweh announced and
then manifested *his sovereign ability* to bring about events.

Again, this is not simply a matter of the Lord possessing information about what was going to take place. It was
rather a matter of the Lord *determining* what was going to
take place and telling his children ahead of time. The verse
doesn't support the view that the future is exhaustively
settled in reality, and thus exhaustively settled in God's
mind.

Openness and Process Thought

Passages such as these beautifully demonstrate that the
future is settled to whatever extent the sovereign Creator
decides to settle it. God is not at the mercy of chance or free
will. This understanding of divine sovereignty contrasts
sharply with a popular liberal theological movement called
"process theology." Some evangelical authors have wrongly
accused open theists of being close to process thought, but
in truth the two views have little in common.[1]

Process thought holds that God *can't* predetermine or
foreknow with certainty *anything* about the distant future.
Open theists rather maintain that God can and does predetermine and foreknow *whatever he wants to* about the future. Indeed, God is so confident in his sovereignty, we
hold, he does not need to micromanage everything. He
could if he wanted to, but this would demean his sovereignty. So he chooses to leave some of the future open to
possibilities, allowing them to be resolved by the decisions
of free agents. It takes a greater God to steer a world populated with free agents than it does to steer a world of preprogrammed automatons.

A Partly Open and Partly Settled Future

The notion that *some* of the future is open while *some* of it is settled seems contradictory to some people. I suspect this is because they are used to thinking in all-or-nothing categories about the future—either the future is totally open or totally settled. Since they are certain from the Word of God that it cannot be totally open, they conclude that it must be totally settled. This all-or-nothing way of thinking about the future is misguided. Far from being contradictory, or even just unusual, the view that the future is *partly* open and *partly* settled is the view we all assume unconsciously every time we make a decision.

For example, I am at the present time deliberating about whether or not I should travel to San Diego next month. In deliberating about this matter, I assume that it is *up to me* to decide when, where, and how I will travel. How could I honestly deliberate about this decision if I didn't believe this? But notice, I *also* assume that much of the future is already settled and not up to me to decide. To deliberate about whether I should travel to San Diego or not, I have to assume that (among many other things) San Diego will exist next month, that the laws of physics will operate as they do today, and that I will be basically the same person then as I am now. I cannot deliberate about issues that are up to me to decide without presupposing the settledness of many other issues that are *not* up to me to decide.

This example illustrates that we cannot consider choices without presupposing that the future is partly open and partly settled—the very position that the open view advocates. If we believed that *all* of the future was open, we could not decide between options. If we believed that *none* of the future was open, we could not decide between options. Hence, the fact that we obviously do decide between options suggests that at some level we all assume that the future is *partly* open and *partly* closed.

The open view simply recognizes this commonsense feature of life and says that it more or less reflects the way things really are. Far from being contradictory, it's the only view that fits with our experience and the Bible's admonitions for us to make godly choices about the future.

Settled Aspects of the Future

Foreknowledge of Israel's Future

Once we understand that the future consists of both open and settled aspects, there is little difficulty understanding how God can foreknow as settled *some* things about the future without assuming that the future is *entirely* settled.

To cite just a few examples, let us grant that for wise reasons God decided to have his chosen people remain in captivity "for four hundred years" (Gen. 15:13–15) in one instance and for "seventy years" in another (Jer. 29:10).[2] Would God have to control and/or foreknow every future decision to ensure this? There is no reason to think that he would.

Consider that none of us chooses where, to whom, or in what socioeconomic class we are born. These matters are decided for us. Yet each of us has a wide range of choices to make within the parameters of these determinations. None of us can choose our mother, for example, but most of us can choose our spouse. Even if we are in a culture where we aren't allowed to choose our spouse, we can choose how we will treat him or her.

We always have choices within parameters of things we do not choose. Lock me up in prison and take away every external freedom I have, and I *still* have a world of choices available to me. Will I love God or not? How will I respond to the temptation to hate, to lust, to despair? Will I pray or not? How will I respond to the harsh treatment of the guards, the spiritual attacks of demons, and the physical discomforts of the prison? How will I respond to the prompting of the Holy Spirit to act and think in godly ways?

Since freedom is always restricted in certain ways, there's no reason to assume that God would have to control or foreknow *all* the future decisions people would make in order to prophesy that the Jews would be in captivity for a particular period of time. This is simply a matter of the Lord defining the parameters within which human freedom will occur.

Individual Prophecies

Many prophecies pertaining to individuals can also be understood as examples of the Lord establishing particular parameters ahead of time. The two most impressive examples of this are Josiah and Cyrus. As a supernatural sign to his people, God named Josiah ("the Lord strengthens") and Cyrus and declared their accomplishments before they were born. This decree obviously set strict parameters around the freedom of the parents in naming these individuals (see also Luke 1:11–23). It also restricted the scope of freedom these individuals could exercise *as it pertained to particular foreordained activities*. In other respects, however, these two individuals and their parents remained self-determining agents.

To conclude from these two examples that the names and activities of *all* people are settled from eternity is unwarranted. They certainly show that Yahweh is the sovereign Lord of history and can predetermine (and thus foreknow) whatever he pleases, but they do not justify the conclusion that he has settled the entire future ahead of time.

Foreknowing Predictable Characters

Sometimes we may understand the Lord's foreknowledge of a person's behavior simply by supposing that the person's character, combined with the Lord's perfect knowledge of all future variables, makes the person's future behavior certain. As we all know, character becomes more predictable over time. The longer we persist in a chosen path, the more that path becomes part of who we are. Hence, generally speaking, the range of viable options we are capable of choosing diminishes over time.

Our omniscient Creator knows us perfectly, far better than we even know ourselves. Hence, we can assume that he is able to predict our behavior far more extensively and accurately than we could predict it ourselves. This does not mean that everything we will ever do is predictable, for our present character doesn't determine all of our future. But it does mean that our behavior is predictable to the extent that our character is solidified and future circumstances that will affect us are in place.

Peter's Denial

Perhaps the most familiar example is when the Lord tells Peter he will deny him three times before morning (Matt. 26:33–35). Contrary to the assumption of many, we do not need to believe that the future is exhaustively settled to explain this prediction. We only need to believe that God the Father knew and revealed to Jesus one very predictable aspect of Peter's character. Anyone who knew Peter's character perfectly could have predicted that under certain highly pressured circumstances (that God could easily orchestrate), he would act just the way he did.[3]

Some have thought that Peter's general bravado, and especially his act of cutting off the ear of the high priest's slave, reveals that his character was not cowardly (Matt. 26:51–52). On the contrary, exposing the superficiality of this bravado was one of the central points of this divinely orchestrated lesson. Peter had just made the typically proud claim to Jesus, "I will never desert you . . . even though I must die" (26:33–34). Jesus told him of his denial at this point in order to set up the disclosure of just how deluded Peter was about both his own character and the character of the Messiah.

It's important to remember that Peter had always believed that the Messiah would be a military leader who would not suffer but rather would vanquish his enemies. Among Jews of the time, this was a common idea. This explains why Peter opposed Jesus' teaching about the need for his sacrificial suffering (see Matt. 16:21–23). It also explains why Peter *appeared* so courageous when the miracle-working Jesus was around but turned into a total coward after Jesus was arrested. His false dream of what Jesus was going to be—and what he would be alongside him—was shattered.

God, of course, saw past Peter's false bravado and knew the effect Jesus' arrest would have on him. He lovingly used this knowledge to teach this important future pillar of the church an invaluable lesson about love and servant leadership. We do not know how much, if any, supernatural intervention was employed in God's orchestration of the events of that evening. But the outcome was just as he anticipated.

Three times Peter had his true character squeezed out of him so that, after the resurrection, he might three times have Christ's character squeezed into him. It is no coincidence that *three times* the resurrected Jesus asked Peter, "Do you love me?" telling him to feed his sheep after each refrain and concluding with a prophecy about how Peter would die a martyr's death, just as he had (John 21:15–19). Never again would Peter identify leadership with military victory. Leadership in the kingdom of God is about laying down one's life and feeding the Lord's sheep. It was a lesson Peter had to learn—and *live*—if he was to be everything God knew he could be.

In any event, it seems evident that we do not need to believe that the future is exhaustively settled in God's mind to make sense of Jesus' prediction of Peter's denial. We need only believe that God possesses a perfect knowledge of the past and present and that he revealed some of it to Jesus.

Judas and the Betrayal of Jesus

I believe that Scripture makes the most sense when we understand Jesus' predictions about Judas's betrayal along similar lines (John 6:64, 70–71; 13:18–19; 17:12). Three things need to be said about Scripture's teachings regarding God's foreknowledge of Judas's betrayal.

First, Scripture says that Jesus knew "from the first" that Judas would betray him (John 6:64). This word (*archē*) does not imply that Jesus knew who would betray him from a time *before* the person decided in his heart to betray him (let alone from all eternity, as the classical view of foreknowledge requires). As in Philippians 4:15, the word can mean "early on." This verse thus suggests that Jesus knew who would betray him from the moment this person resolved to betray him, or from the time Jesus chose him to be a disciple.

Second, many assume that when Jesus referred to Judas as one who was "destined to be lost," he meant that Judas was damned from the beginning of time (John 17:12). However, the verse simply doesn't say this. The Greek translated as "destined to be lost" literally says "son of perdition," with no indication as to *when* Judas had become this. We only know that by the time Jesus said this, Judas had, of his own free will, made himself into a person fit for destruction.[4]

Scripture elsewhere teaches us that a dreadful time may come when God discerns that it is useless to strive with a particular individual or a group of people any longer. At this point, he withdraws his Spirit from these people, hardens their hearts, and thus seals their destinies (e.g., Gen. 6:3; Rom. 1:24–27). When this occurs, the only remaining issue from God's perspective is how he might strategically weave the wicked character of these "sons of perdition" into his divine plan (see Rom. 9:22; Prov. 16:4). By virtue of his self-chosen wickedness, Judas had put himself in just this position. God was now weaving Judas's wickedness into his providential scheme by having him "fulfill" the Scripture about the Messiah being betrayed.

This leads directly to my third point. Jesus tells us that Judas fulfilled Scripture, not that Judas was the one who *had* to fulfill Scripture. We have every reason to suppose that earlier on Judas could have (and should have) chosen a different path for his life, but as a free moral agent, Judas tragically chose a path of self-interest and ultimately self-destruction. If he had made himself into a different kind of person, he would not have been a candidate for fulfilling the prophecy of the Lord's betrayal. In this case, the Lord simply would have found someone else to fill this role.[5]

In my view, this is how we should understand the activity of all the individuals who played prophesied roles in the death of Jesus—e.g., the soldier who pierced his side (John 19:34–37), the soldier who gave him vinegar (John 19:28–29), and the wealthy man who offered his tomb for Jesus' burial (Matt. 27:57–58; cf. Isa. 53:9). Each had acquired a certain kind of character that made him a candidate for the providential use to which the Lord put him. God does not orchestrate that good people carry out evil deeds. He simply specifies parameters around *the way* people act out the good or evil character they have already chosen for themselves.

In any event, we are far outrunning the evidence if we draw the conclusion from these episodes that everything about the future is eternally settled. While it may be difficult to imagine ourselves carrying out a providential plan so masterfully without a meticulous blueprint ahead of time, there is no reason to bring the Lord down to our level. If we grant that God is all-powerful and infinitely wise, we should have no trouble seeing how he could weave free agents into his plan while allowing them to resolve for themselves a partly open future.

Foreknown Life Plans

Our argument has been that the future is partly settled and partly open. The extent to which it is one way or another at any given moment is ultimately decided by God. How does this understanding square with those passages in Scripture that seem to suggest the course of a person's life is determined before they're born, as in the cases of Jeremiah (Jer. 1:5) and Paul (Gal. 1:15)? And how does it square with David's apparent teaching that all the days of his life were written in God's book before he was born (Ps. 139:16)?

Set Apart from the Womb

It is clear from these verses that God had a life plan for Jeremiah and Paul before they were born. This is evidence of exhaustively settled foreknowledge only if Jeremiah and Paul had no choice but to carry out God's plan. Why should we assume this, however? As Paul suggested to King Agrippa, he *could have* chosen to be "disobedient to the heavenly vision" by which he was called (Acts 26:19). This alone suggests that God's "call" on a person's life isn't a guarantee that the person will follow him.

Scripture is filled with examples of people who "rejected God's purpose for themselves" (Luke 7:30). In fact, every sin we have ever committed is an example of resisting God's purposes for our lives, for God doesn't intend us to sin. The same is true of every person who refuses to enter God's eternal kingdom, for God wants "all to come to repentance" and be saved (2 Peter 3:9). The reality of sin and damnation, in other words, demonstrates that God's purposes do not always come about.

Hence, the fact that God intended a course of action for Jeremiah and Paul didn't guarantee that it would come about. Jeremiah and Paul were still free agents, despite God's unique calling on their lives. We know about God's prenatal intentions for these individuals only because they, perhaps unlike others who were called, *did not* disobey this heavenly calling.

Our Days Recorded in God's Book

Is it true that "our days are numbered"? Does David's testimony that "In your book were written all the days that were formed for me" (Ps. 139:16) refute the open view of the future? I'd like to offer four brief considerations in response to this question.

First, even if this verse said that the exact length of our lives was settled before we were born, it wouldn't follow that *everything* about our future was settled before we were born, and certainly not that it was settled from all eternity. God can *at some point* predetermine and/or foreknow *some* things about the future without *eternally* predetermining and/or foreknowing *everything* about the future. We must be careful not to outrun what Scripture teaches.

Second, the fact that the literary form of this verse is poetry should strongly caution us against relying on it to settle doctrinal disputes. The point of this passage is to poetically express God's care for the psalmist from his conception, not to resolve metaphysical disputes regarding the nature of the future.

Third, the Hebrew in this passage is quite ambiguous. First, the word translated in the NRSV as "formed" (*yātsar*) can be interpreted in a strong sense of "determined" or in a weaker sense of "planned." Second, the subject matter of what was "formed" and written in the "book" before they existed is not supplied in the original Hebrew. It is thus not clear whether what was planned were the *days* of the psalmist's life or rather *parts of the psalmist's body*. The King James Version is an example of a translation that decided on the latter meaning. It reads, "Thine eyes did see my substance, yet being unperfect; and in thy book *all my members* were written, which in continuance were fashioned, when as yet there was none of them" (Ps. 139:16). Though this wording is a bit awkward, it has the advantage of being consistent with the rest of this psalm and especially with the immediate context of this verse. Psalm 139 is about God's moment-by-moment, intimate involvement in our lives. The verses immediately preceding verse 16 describe the formation of the psalmist's body in the womb. Indeed, the first stanza of verse 16, "Your eyes beheld my unformed substance," also concerns the intimate awareness the Lord has of the psalmist even before he's formed. An interpretation of this verse that continues this theme seems most appropriate, whereas one that inserts an unrelated reference to the psalmist's future seems out of place.

Finally, even if we choose to take the subject matter of what is "formed" and "written" in this verse to be the days of the psalmist's life (not the parts of his body), this does not require us to believe that the length of his life was unalterable. Scripture elsewhere suggests that what is written in the Lord's Book of Life *can* be changed (Exod. 32:33; Rev. 3:5). Hezekiah's success in getting the Lord to "add" fifteen years to his life supports this perspective (Isa. 38:1–5), as does the Lord's self-professed willingness to alter decrees he's made in light of new circumstances (Jer. 18:6–10). The notion that what God ordains is necessarily unalterable is foreign to the Hebrew mind.

In the context of the whole counsel of Scripture, it seems best to understand the term *yātsar* as well as the writing in God's "book" as referring to God's *intentions* at the time of the psalmist's fetal development, not an unalterable decree of God.

Prophecies of Kingdoms and Judgments

Choose Your Own Adventure

What about biblical passages that speak of the future movements of nations, such as the four successive kingdoms mentioned in Nebuchadnezzar's dream (Dan. 2:38–40)? The open view "explains" this and every other passage of Scripture that relates to the future by simply accepting that the future is settled to the extent that the passage in question says it is settled, no more or no less. Where the open view and the classical view differ in their treatment of passages such as these is that the open view does not read into these verses the *assumption* that the future must be exhaustively settled.

This passage certainly presupposes that the succession and relative strengths of several future kingdoms was settled at the time of Nebuchadnezzar's dream. But the verse does not say that everything about the future, or everything about these particular kingdoms, was settled. As we noted earlier, freedom is always restricted within parameters set by God and other factors.

An overly simple but clear analogy of the open view of providence might be the children's "Choose Your Own Adventure" stories. In these stories, an author writes a number of possible plotlines and allows readers to create their own story by choosing between alternatives. The author provides a structure to the story as a whole and to each possible plotline within the overall structure. But within these predefined parameters, there is room for readers to create their own stories by choosing between the options that the author has given.

This is a model (albeit, infinitely simplified) of how we may understand God's sovereign design allowing for some openness in the future, both at an individual and at a national level. The God of the possible is the author of the whole story line of creation and the one who offers possible alternatives to his human and angelic creations. The rise and fall of nations is to some extent providentially guided according to God's plans for world history (see Dan. 2:21). But within this general guidance, there is plenty of room for individuals to exercise free will.

Ordaining National Boundaries

This is also how we should understand Paul's teaching that God "made all nations to inhabit the whole earth, and he allotted the times of their existence and the boundaries of the places where they would live" (Acts 17:26). This is part of the structural outline of God's plan for world history. These providential parameters certainly *condition* the scope of human freedom, but they do not eliminate it—just as our genes and environment condition our individual freedom without eliminating it.

44

Paul himself says that God establishes these national parameters with the hope "that they [the nations] would search for God and *perhaps* grope for him and find him" (Acts 17:27). There is ordained structure balanced by freedom. God determines whatever he sees fit and leaves as much of the future open to possibilities as he sees fit. The God of the possible creates the "Choose Your Own Adventure" structure of world history and of our lives within which the possibilities of human free choice are actualized.

The Openness of Biblical Prophecy

One other aspect of the parameters that God establishes around nations, cities, and individuals needs to be mentioned. Scripture demonstrates that these parameters are often flexible. As we will explore more fully in the next chapter, the Lord tells us that even after he has prophesied for or against a nation, he will "change [his] mind" if the nation changes (Jer. 18:1–12). We find many examples of this "changing" occurring at national and individual levels. Thus, even when the Lord announces that some aspect of the future is settled, it may still be alterable. The "settledness" may be conditioned on unsettled factors, such as decisions we make.

What this shows us is that not only is part of the future open, but also some aspects of the future that God has announced as settled are to some extent open. God's mind can yet be changed, a biblical truth that is difficult to square with the classical view of divine foreknowledge.

The Foreordained Messiah and the Predestined Church
Predestined Event with Non-Predestined Players

Since God determines whatever he wants to about world history, we should not find it surprising that the central defining event in world history—the crucifixion—included a number of predestined aspects. It seems that the incarnation and crucifixion were part of God's plan from "before the foundation of the world" (1 Peter 1:20; cf. Rev. 13:8). Hence, Scripture makes it clear that Jesus was not crucified by accident. Rather, he was delivered up and crucified "according to the definite plan and foreknowledge of God" (Acts 2:23; see also 4:28).

While Scripture portrays the crucifixion as a predestined event, it never suggests that the individuals who participated in this event were predestined to do so or foreknown as doing so. It was certain that Jesus would be crucified, but it was not certain from eternity that Pilot, Herod, or Caiaphas would play the roles they played in the crucifixion. They participated in Christ's death of their own free wills.

Freedom and Determinism in Science and Life

Some scholars have argued that it is not possible for God to predestine an event without predestining or at least foreknowing the people who would carry out the event. There is no justification for limiting God in this fashion, however. Indeed, many branches of contemporary science are founded on the idea that things can be somewhat predictable while incorporating unpredictable elements.

For example, contemporary physics has taught us that we can accurately predict the general behavior of a group of quantum particles, but not the exact behavior of any individual particle. Chaos theory also has taught us that all predictable aspects of reality incorporate unpredictable aspects. This balance between predictable and unpredictable aspects of reality is illustrated in many areas of our everyday lives. For example, though insurance and advertising agencies make money by utilizing statistics to predict gen-

46

eral group behavior, they are still incapable of predicting individual behavior. They have learned how to capitalize on what social scientists and anthropologists have been telling us for some time—namely, that group behavior is far more predictable than individual behavior. We can, for example, accurately predict that between 7 and 8 percent of fourteen-year-olds will take up smoking this year. But we cannot tell *which individuals* will comprise this 7 to 8 percent.

In this light, it should not be difficult to understand how God could predestine the crucifixion without predestining or foreknowing who, specifically, would carry it out. To put the matter crudely, God would simply have to possess a perfect version of what insurance and advertising agencies possess. He would have to know that a certain percentage of people (and perhaps fallen angels, see Luke 22:3; John 13:27; 1 Cor. 2:8) in authoritative positions would act in certain ways under certain circumstances.[6]

The Predestined Church

In the same way that God predestined and foreknew the death of Jesus without predestining or foreknowing which individuals would condemn him, so God predestined and foreknew the church without predestining or foreknowing which specific individuals would belong to it. A careful examination of the relevant texts supports this interpretation.

For example, when Paul says that God "chose us in Christ before the foundation of the world," he immediately specifies that this predestination was for us "to be holy and blameless before him in love" (Eph. 1:4). Note, Paul does *not* say that we were *individually* predestined to be "in Christ" (or not). Scripture elsewhere tells us that if it were up to God alone, he would save everyone (1 Tim. 2:4; 2 Peter

3:9). But it is not up to God alone; God gave humans free will. What Paul says in this verse is that *whoever chooses* to be "in Christ" is predestined to be "holy and blameless before him in love." Now that we have chosen to be "in Christ," we can say with Paul that *"we* [believers] were predestined to be holy and blameless" before God. Indeed, as a group we were given this grace "in Christ Jesus before the ages began" (2 Tim. 1:9).

Consider this analogy: Suppose you attend a seminar in which a certain video is shown. You might ask the instructor, "When was it decided (predestined) that we'd watch this video?" To which the instructor might respond, "It was decided six months ago that you'd watch this video." Note that it was not decided six months ago that *you individually* would watch this video. What was decided was that *anyone who took this seminar* would watch this video. Now that you have chosen to be part of this seminar, what was predestined for the seminar applies to you. You can now say, "It was decided six months ago that *we* would watch this video."

This is what Paul meant when he said that we were predestined in Christ "to be holy and blameless before him in love." Now that you are a believer who is "in Christ," what was predestined for all who are "in Christ" is predestined for you.

Foreloved and Predestined

Something similar must be said about Paul's statement that "those whom [God] foreknew he also predestined to be conformed to the image of his Son" (Rom. 8:29). Many interpret this verse to mean that God foreknew that certain individuals would believe and then predestined them to be conformed to the image of his Son. But we must notice that Paul doesn't specify that God foreknew certain individuals would believe. He simply says, "those whom [God] foreknew he also predestined." We must be careful not to read into the verse more than is there.

Now, if by "foreknowledge" Paul meant to refer to certain information about the future that God possessed, this passage would present a serious problem to the classical view of divine foreknowledge. For the verse clearly contrasts "those whom God foreknew" with others God did *not* foreknow. But in the classical view of foreknowledge, of course, God foreknows with certainty everything about everyone throughout the whole of the future. There is nothing for God's foreknowledge to contrast with.

There is no reason to think that Paul has information in mind when he speaks of God's foreknowledge, however. In customary Semitic fashion, Paul seems to be using the word *know* to mean "intimately love." This is clearly his meaning when, two chapters later, he refers to Israel as the people "whom [God] foreknew" (Rom. 11:2). In this context, Paul has Israel *as a corporate whole* in mind, not individual Jews, for one of his primary goals throughout Romans 9–11 is to show that not all Jews are real Israelites. Israel was in God's affection and plan long before she became a nation—she was foreloved—even though at the time Paul was writing most of the Jews individually had rejected God's plan.

So too, in Romans 8:29 Paul is saying that the church as a corporate whole was in God's heart long before the church was birthed. But this doesn't imply that he knew who would and would not be in this church ahead of time. He predestined that all who choose to receive Christ would grow to be in the image of his Son. But whether particular individuals receive Christ and thus acquire this predestined image depends on their free will.

End Times Prophecies

When Are the "Last Days"?

Finally, a word should be said about the end times prophecies mentioned earlier. It is important to remember that New Testament authors uniformly considered themselves to be living "in the last days" (Acts 2:17; Heb. 1:2; 1 Peter 1:20). They weren't mistaken in thinking this way, but the period covered by the phrase "last days" has obviously turned out to be longer than they expected (2 Peter 3:7–10). This observation is important because when the New Testament speaks about issues related to "the last days," some are prone to think it is referring to our present age, not theirs. In reality, however, it is referring to both. Hence, when Paul talks about people who "in later times" pay attention to "deceitful spirits" (1 Tim. 4:1–3), we must understand that he is speaking about his own day as well as ours. Clearly, passages such as these present no challenge to the open view of the future.

Many exegetes argue that Paul's reference to the great "rebellion" and "the lawless one" who would exalt himself above God (2 Thess. 2:3–4) also refer to events that were to take place in Paul's own day (e.g., the destruction of Jerusalem in A.D. 70). Whether this is accepted or not, this passage does not rule out the possibility of the future being somewhat open. It simply assumes that God knows the character of Satan well enough to predict some of his strategy at the end of the age when he releases his fury one final time.

The Book of Revelation

Finally, a word must be said about the Book of Revelation. As mentioned earlier, many contemporary readers (unlike most readers throughout history) believe this book is about events that will take place at the end of history.

Even if we accept this way of interpreting Revelation, it does not require that we believe that the future is exhaustively settled. The primary actors in this apocalyptic narrative are God and Satan, and it's not hard to understand how God could know very well the plans of both at the end of history without supposing that *all* of the future is settled in God's mind.

There are very good arguments against interpreting the Book of Revelation in this way, however. Most importantly, this reading of Revelation violates one of the most fundamental principles of sound biblical exegesis: Namely, the primary meaning of any text is *the meaning the text would have had to its original audience.*

John tells us he is writing to "the seven churches that are in Asia" (1:4) about events that "must *soon* take place" (1:1) because "the time is *near*" (1:3; see also 22:6, 10). Throughout this book, there is an emphasis on the nearness of the events it depicts and the need for readers to respond quickly (see 2:16; 3:10–11; 22:6, 7, 12, 20). To understand Revelation properly, therefore, we should hear it read aloud to us (see 1:3)—rather than meticulously combing through with a decoding agenda, as some contemporary interpreters do. We must, as much as possible, try to understand this book as a first-century Christian in Asia Minor would understand it.

When we do this, we find that most of the symbols used throughout this work have their origin in the Old Testament and their primary application in the first century. For example, it is easy to see the emperor Nero as "the beast," since the name "Nero Caesar" in Hebrew *(nrwn qsr)* adds up to 666 (13:18). Moreover, the forty-two months of his horrifying reign (13:5) turns out to be the exact duration of the Roman siege on Jerusalem beginning in A.D. 66.

The basic message of this heavily symbolic book, however, applies to all times and all places. God is in the process of defeating his foe and judging the world. Hence, believers should take courage and persevere in the face of persecution.[7]

If this interpretation is accepted, there is no difficulty reconciling this book with the view that the future is partly open.

Conclusion

This chapter has examined the motif in Scripture that expresses and celebrates God's control and foreknowledge of the future. We have seen that Scripture portrays God as the omniscient, sovereign Lord of history. He decrees whatever he wishes to decree. He controls whatever he chooses to control. He is never caught off guard or at a loss of options. He anticipates and ingeniously outmaneuvers his opponents. Hence, all who align themselves with him can have total confidence that he will ultimately achieve his objectives for creation.

We have also seen, however, that the passages that express this motif do not require us to believe that the future is exhaustively settled. To confess that God can control whatever he wants to control leaves open the question of *how much* God actually does want to control. If Scripture warrants it, there is "room" within this motif for the belief that some of the future is not determined, and thus not foreknown as settled by God. In the next chapter, we will argue that Scripture not only warrants this conclusion, it requires it.

TWO

The God Who Faces
a Partially Open Future

Thus far we have examined the motif of Scripture that celebrates God's sovereignty over creation and lordship over history. God predestines and foreknows as settled whatever he sees fit to predestine and foreknow as settled. We have also seen, however, that this motif of future determinism does not warrant the conclusion that God predestines and foreknows as settled *everything* about the future. As we will see in this chapter, there is a second major motif in Scripture that depicts the future as partly open. Balancing the determined aspects of the future is a realm composed of open possibilities that will be resolved only by the decisions of free agents.

If the motif of future determinism required the view that the future were *exhaustively* settled, as the classical view of foreknowledge argues, Scripture would seem to contradict itself. Obviously, the future can't be *both* partly open *and* exhaustively settled. As noted in the introduction, the classical view attempts to avoid this contradiction by claiming that the second motif in Scripture is nonliteral. If we accept the findings of the previous chapter that the motif of future determinism only requires us to view the future as *partly* settled, however, there is no contradiction. We are free to accept and celebrate both motifs in Scripture as telling us important truths about God and the nature of the future.

The open view is rooted in the conviction that the passages that constitute the motif of future openness should be taken just as literally as the passages that constitute the motif of future determinism. For this reason, the open view concludes that the future is literally settled to whatever degree God wants to settle it, and literally open to the extent that God desires to leave it open to be resolved by the decisions of his creations. This view, open theists argue, is truer to the whole counsel of Scripture, truer to our experience, and offers a number of theological and practical advantages as well (see chapters 3 and 4).

The goal of this chapter is to examine the scriptural motif of future openness. Because of the dominance of the classical view of foreknowledge with its overemphasis on the motif of future determinism, much of this material may be unfamiliar to the reader. However, this material is just as much a part of the inspired Word of God and needs to be taken just as seriously as more familiar passages. I will argue that the passages that constitute this motif strongly suggest that the future is partly open and that God knows it as such.

I will also argue that the classical explanation—that these verses are less literal than those expressing future determinism—is unwarranted.

For our present purposes, it will be helpful to break down the motif of future openness into several sections.

God Regrets How Things Turn Out

God's Regret Regarding Pre-Flood Humanity

To begin, one aspect of the portrait of God in Scripture that suggests the future is partly open is the fact that God sometimes regrets how things turn out, even prior decisions that *he himself made*. For example, in the light of the depravity that characterized humanity prior to the flood, the Bible says that "The LORD *was sorry* that he had made humankind on the earth, and it grieved him to his heart" (Gen. 6:6). The genuineness of his regret is evidenced by the fact that the Lord immediately took measures to destroy humanity and start over.

Now, if everything about world history were exhaustively settled and known by God as such before he created the world, God would have known with absolute certainty that humans would come to this wicked state, at just this time, before he created them. But how, then, could he authentically regret having made humankind? Doesn't the fact that God regretted the way things turned out—to the point of starting over—suggest that it *wasn't* a foregone conclusion at the time God created human beings that they would fall into this state of wickedness?

God's Regret over Saul's Kingship

Another fascinating example of the Lord's regret concerns his decision to make Saul king of Israel. While having a king was never God's first choice, the appointment of Saul could have worked out well. Indeed, Scripture tells us that God had intended to bless him and his household for many generations (1 Sam 13:13).

Unfortunately, Saul chose to forsake God's ways and to pursue his own agenda. When Saul's heart changed, God's plan for him changed; he was no longer going to bless Saul. Instead, God removed him from his appointed office and allowed his sin to take its course. Saul had gotten so wicked that the Lord said, "I *regret* that I made Saul king, for he has turned back from following me" (1 Sam. 15:10). The point is reiterated for emphasis several verses later, when Scripture says, "the LORD *was sorry* that he had made Saul king over Israel" (1 Sam. 15:35).

We must wonder how the Lord could truly experience regret for making Saul king if he was absolutely certain that Saul would act the way he did. Could God genuinely confess, "I regret that I made Saul king" if he could in the same breath also proclaim, "I was certain of what Saul would do when I made him king"? I do not see how. Could I genuinely regret, say, purchasing a car because it turned out to run poorly if in fact the car was running exactly as I knew it would when I purchased it? Common sense tells us that we can only regret a decision we made if the decision resulted in an outcome other than what we expected or hoped for when the decision was made.

Does Regret Imply Lack of Wisdom?

Now some may object that if God regretted a decision he made, he must not be perfectly wise. Wouldn't God be admitting to making a mistake? Two considerations lead me to answer this question in the negative.

First, it is better to allow Scripture to inform us regarding the nature of divine wisdom than to reinterpret an entire motif in order to square it with our preconceptions of divine wisdom. If God says he regretted a decision, and if Scripture elsewhere tells us that God is perfectly wise, then we should simply conclude that one can be perfectly wise and still regret a decision. Even if this is a mystery to us, it is better to allow the mystery to stand than to assume that we know what God's wisdom is like and conclude on this basis that God can't mean what he clearly says.

My second point, however, is that in the open view there is little mystery involved in accepting that God can regret his own previous decisions. Once we understand that the future is partly open and that humans are genuinely free, the paradox of how God could experience genuine regret over a decision he made disappears. God made a wise decision because it had the greatest *possibility* of yielding the best results. God's decision wasn't the only variable in this matter, however; there was also the variable of Saul's will. Saul freely strayed from God's plan, but that is not God's fault, nor does it make God's decision unwise.

The God Who Risks

A wise risk is a risk nonetheless. It may not turn out as one hopes. Classical theologians, however, generally reject the notion that God takes risks of any sort. To them, it undermines his sovereignty. Two further considerations address this charge.

First, don't we normally regard someone who refuses to take risks as being insecure? Don't we ordinarily regard a compulsion to meticulously control everything as evidencing weakness, not strength? Of course we do. Everyone who is psychologically healthy knows it is good to risk loving another person, for example. You may, of course, get hurt, for people are free agents. But the risk-free alternatives of not loving or of trying to control another person is evidence of insecurity and weakness, if not sickness. Why should we abandon this insight when we think about God, especially since Scripture clearly depicts God as sometimes taking risks?

Second, the only way to deny that God takes risks is to maintain that *everything* that occurs in world history is *exactly* what God *wanted* to occur. If anything is other than what God wanted, to that extent he obviously risked not getting what he wanted when he created the world. So, if God is truly "above" taking risks, then we must accept that things such as sin, child mutilations, and people going to hell are all in accordance with God's will.

Remarkably, some believers are willing to follow their logic to this stunning conclusion, but the vast majority of Christians reject it in horror. God is "not wanting *any* to perish, but all to come to repentance" (2 Peter 3:9). Note, however, that this means that most Christians already believe that God *doesn't* always get his way. And logically this means most Christians must accept that God took risks when he created the world. Among other things, every time he created free moral agents he took the risk that they might choose to destroy themselves by rejecting him.

God's risks are always wise, of course, for the possibility of things going God's way is worth it. But they are risks nonetheless. In a cosmos populated by free agents, the outcome of things—even divine decisions—is often uncertain.

God Asks Questions about the Future

A second aspect of the portrait of God in Scripture that may suggest the future is partially open is that God sometimes expresses uncertainty about it. For example, he asks Moses, "How long will this people despise me? And how long will they refuse to believe in me, in spite of all the signs that I have done among them?" (Num. 14:11). Similarly, we later read of God asking Hosea, "How long will they [Israel] be incapable of innocence?" (Hosea 8:5; cf. 1 Kings 22:20). If God wonders about future issues, does this not imply that the future is to some extent unsettled?

Some suggest that in these verses the Lord was asking rhetorical questions, just as he had done when he asked Adam and Eve where they were (Gen. 3:8–9). This is a possible interpretation, but not a necessary one. Unlike God's question about location in Genesis, there is nothing in these texts or in the whole of Scripture that requires these questions to be rhetorical. Moreover, the fact that the Lord continued for centuries, with much frustration, to try to get the Israelites not to "despise" him and to be "innocent" suggests that the wonder expressed in these questions was genuine. The duration of the Israelites' stubbornness was truly an open issue.

God Confronts the Unexpected

Surprise at "Wild Grapes"

Third, sometimes God tells us that things turn out differently than he expected. For example, in Isaiah 5 the Lord describes Israel as his vineyard and himself as its loving owner. He explains that, as the owner of the vineyard, he "*expected* it to yield grapes, but it yielded wild grapes" (v. 2). He then asks, "What more was there to do for my vineyard that I have not done in it? When I *expected* it to yield grapes, why did it yield wild grapes?" (v. 4). Because it unexpectedly failed to yield grapes, the Lord sadly concludes, "I will remove its hedge, and it shall be devoured" (v. 5).

If everything is eternally certain to God, as the classical view of foreknowledge holds, how could the Lord twice say that he "expected" one thing to occur, only to have something different occur? How could the Lord expect, hope for, and even strive ("what more was there to do?") for something he knew from all eternity would never happen? If we take the passage at face value, does it not imply that the future of Israel, the "vineyard," was not certain until they settled it by choosing to yield "wild grapes"?

"I Thought You'd Return"

Several other examples of the Lord confronting the unexpected are found in Jeremiah. Beholding Israel's remarkable obstinacy, the Lord says, "I *thought*, 'After she has done all this she will return to me'; but she did not return" (Jer. 3:6–7). He repeats his dismay to Israel several verses later: "I *thought* how I would set you among my children.... And I *thought* you would call me, 'My Father,' and would not turn from following me. Instead, as a faithless wife ... you have been faithless to me" (Jer. 3:19–20).

We need to ask ourselves seriously, how could the Lord honestly say he *thought* Israel would turn to him if he was always certain that they would never do so? If God tells us he thought something was going to occur while being eternally certain it would not occur, is he not lying to us? If God cannot lie (Heb. 6:18) and yet tells us he thought something would occur that did not occur, doesn't this imply that the future contains possibilities as well as certainties?

Some have tried to avoid this conclusion by pointing out that the Hebrew word *āmar* can be translated as "said." But this doesn't help the classical view of divine foreknowledge. It only transfers the problem of God *thinking* something was going to happen that didn't happen, to him *saying* he expected something to happen that he knew would not happen.

Infallibly Knowing Probabilities

Do these verses imply that God is mistaken? They certainly do if you assume that the future is exhaustively settled ahead of time. In this case, God would be *wrong* for expecting one thing to occur when it was a settled fact that another thing was certainly going to occur. But no mistake is implied if you believe that the future is partly open.

If the future consists in part of possibilities, then God can infallibly think that a particular possibility has the greatest chance of occurring, even if it turns out that a less likely possibility actually occurs. Since God is omniscient, he always knew that it was remotely possible for his people to be this stubborn, for example. But he genuinely did not expect them to actualize this remote possibility. He authentically expected that they'd be won over by his grace. God wasn't caught off guard (for he knew this stubbornness was possible), but he was genuinely disappointed (for he knew the possibility was improbable and hoped it wouldn't come to pass).

The open view of God can thus understand these verses without detracting in any way from God's omniscience. If the future is exhaustively settled in God's mind, however, then no clear sense can be made out of these verses, for there are no real possibilities to God; there are only certainties. In the classical view, God's expectations can never be different from what transpires.

It "Never Entered My Mind"

Several other passages in Jeremiah confirm this. Three times the Lord expresses shock over Israel's ungodly behavior by saying that they were doing things "which I did not command or decree, *nor did it enter my mind*" (Jer. 19:5; see also 7:31; 32:35). However we understand the phrase "nor did it enter my mind," it would at the very least seem to preclude the possibility that the Israelites' idolatrous behavior was eternally certain in God's mind. If the classical view is correct, we have to be willing to accept that God could in one breath say that the Israelites' behavior "did not enter my mind," though their behavior "was eternally in my mind." If this is not a contradiction, what is?

God Gets Frustrated

The fourth aspect of the motif of future openness is that throughout Scripture we find God being frustrated as people stubbornly resist his plans for their lives. This dominant feature of the biblical narrative is hard to square with the view that the entire future is eternally settled. Think about it. How could the Lord genuinely be frustrated trying to achieve things he is certain all along will not come to pass?

For example, several times the Lord tried to convince Moses that he could use him despite his speech impediment. Moses repeatedly refused to accept this (Exod. 4:10–15). Finally, Scripture says, "the anger of the LORD was kindled against Moses and he said, 'What of your brother Aaron, the Levite? I know he can speak fluently'" (v. 14). God was clearly frustrated by Moses' persistent unbelief. If it was a foregone conclusion that Moses would *not* go along with God's plan, however, one wonders why God frustrated himself trying to get Moses to do so.

Another example of the Lord's frustration is found in Ezekiel, as the Lord mournfully declares the judgment he is bringing upon Israel. The Lord says, "I *sought* for anyone among them who would repair the wall and stand in the breach before me on behalf of the land, so that I would not destroy it: but I found no one. Therefore I have poured out my indignation upon them" (Ezek. 22:30–31).

This passage is one of the strongest depictions of the re-markable power and awesome responsibility of prayer. It suggests that if God could have found "anyone" to pray, judgment on the nation of Israel would have been averted. But although God tried to find someone to "stand in the breach," he found no one. This episode stands in stark contrast to the many other episodes in Scripture in which God's plan to bring judgment *was* reversed through the power of prayer (see Exod. 32:14; Num. 11:1–2; 14:12–20; 16:20–35, 41–48; Deut. 9:13–14, 18–20, 25; Judg. 10:13–16; 2 Sam. 24:17–25; 1 Kings 21:21–29; 2 Kings 13:3–5; 20:1–6; 2 Chron. 12:5–8).

In any event, it is difficult to understand how God could have sincerely "sought for" someone to intercede if he was eternally certain that there would be no one. Could you genuinely look for a coin in your house that you always *knew* was not there? The fact that God *tried* to raise up an intercessor suggests that he knew it was *possible* that an intercessor would have responded. But this requires us to believe that it was *not* certain to God that there would be no intercessor when he sought one. And this means that the future must partly be composed of possibilities, not certainties.

God Tests People to Know Their Character

The fifth and strongest group of passages we've examined thus far that suggest the future is not exhaustively settled shows that God frequently tests his covenant partners to see if they will choose to follow him or not.

Testing and Covenantal Faithfulness

This testing isn't a game for God. It lies at the heart of God's call to keep covenant with him. He creates us free, for his goal is love, and love must be chosen. It cannot be preprogrammed. And so from the very beginning (Genesis 3), God's call to covenantal faithfulness has involved testing. God is seeking to *find out* whether or not the people he calls will lovingly choose him above all else.

However, if the future is exhaustively settled, and if God foreknows the future only in terms of certainties, never possibilities, then there is nothing for God to "find out." Defenders of the classical view argue that the purpose of divine testing wasn't for *God* to find out how his covenant partners would behave, but for *the covenant partners* to find out something about themselves. Unfortunately for this view, this is not at all how Scripture describes the matter.

Testing "to Know" One's Fidelity

When Abraham successfully passed God's test by being willing to offer up his son Isaac, the Lord declared, "*Now* I know that you fear God, *since* you have not withheld your son" (Gen. 22:12). The verse clearly says that it was *because* Abraham did what he did that the Lord *now* knew he was a faithful covenant partner. The verse has no clear meaning if God was certain that Abraham would fear him before he offered up his son.

Similarly, the Bible says that God tested Hezekiah "*to know* all that was in his heart*" (2 Chron. 32:31). If God eternally knew how Hezekiah would respond to him, God couldn't have *really* been testing him in order to come to this knowledge. Unfortunately for the classical view, however, this is exactly what the text says.

Corporate Testing

In keeping with Scripture's depiction of corporate election, many of the "testing" passages of Scripture concern the behavior of Israel as a whole. For example, Moses tells the Israelites that the Lord kept them in the desert for forty years "in order to humble you, testing you *to know* what was in your heart, whether or not you would keep his commandments" (Deut. 8:2). Elsewhere he told the Israelites that the Lord allowed false prophets to be correct sometimes because he "is testing you, *to know* whether you indeed love the LORD your God with all your heart and soul" (Deut. 13:1–3).

In another instance, the Lord withheld assistance to Israel in battle "in order to test Israel, *whether or not* they would take care to walk in the way of the LORD as their ancestors did" (Judg. 2:22). He left Israel's opponents alone, Scripture says, "for the testing of Israel, *to know* whether Israel would obey the commandments of the LORD" (Judg. 3:4). And, finally, the Lord commanded the Israelites to gather only enough bread from heaven for one day while they walked in the wilderness in order to "test them *whether* they will follow my instruction *or not*" (Exod. 16:4).

Note carefully, these verses do not say that the purpose of the testing was for the covenant partners to know *their own* hearts. The explicitly stated purpose was for *God* "to know" how they would incline their hearts. How can this be reconciled with the view that God eternally knows exactly what will be in the heart of a person to do? How is it compatible with the classical assumption that God never comes to know anything, for his knowledge is unchanging? I see no viable way of reconciling this view with Scripture.

If we accept that the future is partly open, however, and if free agents resolve their hearts only when they decide on a course of action, then these verses make perfect sense. Except in cases in which a solidified character or God's predestining plan makes people predictable (see chapter 1), Scripture teaches us that God literally finds out *how* people will choose *when* they choose. He made us self-determining agents, and prior to our determining ourselves in one direction or another, the only reality that exists for God to know concerning our future action is the possible directions we may take.

Divine Testing and Divine Disappointment

It's also interesting to note that many times the outcomes of these tests were not what God hoped for. For example, Psalm 95:10–11 and Hebrews 3:7–10 describe God's frustration with Israel regarding their hardness toward him "on the day of testing" (Heb. 3:8). This raises the question as to why God strove with Israel for forty years and then for centuries after they entered the Promised Land if he was certain from the outset that they would grieve him (see Eph. 4:30)? Why test someone you know will flunk—and then experience grief over the flunking—when you were certain ahead of time what would happen?

The fact that God tested people "to know" their behavior suggests that he didn't know what they'd choose ahead of time, and that it was, from God's vantage point, genuinely *possible* for these people to pass (or fail) the test.

God Speaks in Terms of What *May* or *May Not* Be

Sixth, the motif of future openness is expressed by the way the Lord often talks about the future in Scripture. If everything was settled in God's mind from all eternity as the classical view holds, you would expect God to speak of the future in absolute terms. There would be no "maybes" for God. Remarkably, however, the Bible records numerous examples of God speaking in terms of what *might* or *might not* happen. Since God is omniscient and knows reality exactly as it is, these passages suggest that the future consists in part of things that might or might not happen.

They "May" Believe

One of the most interesting examples of this is when God tries to convince Moses to be his representative to the elders of Israel who are in bondage to Pharaoh. The Lord initially tells Moses that the elders will listen to his voice (Exod. 3:18). Moses apparently doesn't hold to the classical view of divine foreknowledge, however, for he immediately asks, "suppose they do not believe me or listen to me?" (Exod. 4:1).

God's response to him suggests that God doesn't hold to this view of foreknowledge either. He first demonstrates a miracle "so that they may believe that the LORD . . . has appeared to you" (4:5). Moses remains unconvinced, so the Lord performs a second miracle and comments, "*If* they will not believe you or heed the first sign, they *may* believe the second sign" (4:8). How can the Lord say, "they *may* believe"? Isn't the future behavior of the elders a matter of certainty for the Lord? Apparently not. Indeed, the Lord continues, "*If* they will not believe even these two signs or heed you, you shall take some water from the Nile and pour it on the dry ground; and the water that you shall take from the Nile will become blood on the dry ground" (4:9).

If the future is exhaustively settled, God would of course have known exactly how many miracles, if any, it would take to get the elders to believe Moses. In that case, the meaning of the words he chose ("may," "if") could not be sincere. If we believe that God speaks straightforwardly, however, it seems he did not foreknow with certainty exactly how many miracles it would take to get the elders of Israel to believe Moses.

This verse demonstrates that God is perfectly confident in his ability to achieve the results he is looking for (getting the elders of Israel to listen to Moses) even though he works with free agents who are, to some extent, unpredictable. That the Israelites would get out of Egypt was certain; how many miracles it would take to pull this off depended on the free choices of some key people. This is a picture of a God who is as creative and resourceful as he is wise and powerful.

The Glory of True Divine Sovereignty

As noted in the previous chapter, we have difficulty fathoming such a creative, wise, and lovingly powerful sovereignty. And this, perhaps, explains why many are inclined to assume that God needs an exhaustive blueprint of what is coming in order to accomplish his purposes. If we simply allow biblical texts to say what they seem to say, however, we are led to embrace the conclusion that God is *so* wise, resourceful, and sovereign over history that he doesn't need or want to have everything in the future settled ahead of time. He is *so* confident in his power and wisdom that he is willing to grant an appropriate degree of freedom to humans (and angels) to determine their own futures.

In my view, every other understanding of divine providence to some extent diminishes the sovereignty and glory of God. It brings God's wisdom and power down to the level of finite human thinking. *We* would need to control or possess a blueprint of all that is to occur ahead of time to steer world history effectively. But the true God is far wiser, far more powerful, and far more secure than we could ever imagine.

Remember whom we are speaking about. This is the omnipotent Creator who "flexes his omnipotent muscle," as it were, by being born in a stable, growing up with the stigma of being an illegitimate child, hanging out with sinners, and dying a God-forsaken death on the cross! To the natural understanding, this is foolishness, but to the apostle Paul, it is the wisdom and power of God (1 Cor. 1:18). This demonstrates that the normal human way of thinking about sovereignty only as control is misguided (see Matt. 20:25–28). God is *so* sovereign, he chooses to save the world by allowing himself to become weak.

Since Jesus is for believers the very definition of God (John 1:18; 14:7–10; Heb. 1:3), we must not think of the cross as an exception to the way God really is. Rather, the cross constitutes the supreme example of the way God is. God rules by love, not control. God's unchanging gracious character leads him to change in response to us. God's glory is displayed in his allowing himself to be affected by us. And God's sovereignty partly consists in his openness to us and to the future we help create.

Speaking in Conditional Terms

We have been arguing that the way God speaks about the future in conditional terms is evidence that the future is partly open. It may prove helpful to provide just a few more examples of this pervasive tendency.

In Exodus 13:17, for example, we learn that the Lord decided against leading Israel along the shortest route to Canaan because Israel would have had to fight the Philistines. The Lord thought it best to avoid this, saying, "*Lest* the people change their minds when they see war, and they return to Egypt." The New International Version translates this, "*If* they face war they *might* change their minds and return to Egypt." If we accept this language as inspired by God, doesn't it clearly imply that God considered the *possibility,* but not the *certainty,* that the Israelites would change their minds if they faced battle?

In an even more impressive example, the Lord had Ezekiel symbolically enact Israel's exile as a warning, telling

him, "*Perhaps* they will understand, though they are a re-
bellious house" (Ezek. 12:3). As it turns out, Israel did not
"understand." If God was certain all along that Israel would
not understand, how can we avoid the conclusion that he
was *lying* when he told Ezekiel they *might* understand? Indeed, if the "perhaps" that the Lord spoke didn't indicate a
real possibility to God, one wonders what the point of this
symbolic enactment was in the first place.

Similarly, the Lord commanded Jeremiah to preach to
the cities of Judah, telling him, "It *may* be that they will listen . . . and will turn from their evil way, that I may change
my mind about the disaster that I intend to bring on them
because of their evil doings" (Jer. 26:3). Jeremiah's preaching did not bring about the result God hoped for, which
leads to this question: If God was certain the Judeans would
not repent, was he not lying when he led Jeremiah to believe that they *might* repent? Indeed, if God never really
changes his mind, was he not misleading Jeremiah and all
the people by encouraging them to think of him as one who
might change his mind (see Jer. 26:19)?

If we hold that the future is somewhat open, then passages such as these make perfect sense. When God gave
Ezekiel and Jeremiah their assignments, there was at least
a *chance* that people would respond favorably to them. God
knows all of reality exactly as it is, so God had a perfect
knowledge of what this chance was. He spoke genuinely
when he told Ezekiel and Jeremiah that the people might
understand and repent. The fact that the Israelites refused
to understand or repent simply explains why God said "perhaps" and "maybe" instead of "surely."

"If It Is Possible"

Yet another impressive example of the Lord speaking
about the future in open terms is found in Jesus' prayer in

the Garden of Gethsemane. Jesus "threw himself on the ground and prayed, 'My Father, if it is possible, let this cup pass from me'" (Matt. 26:39). As we saw in the previous chapter, if anything was fixed in the mind of God ahead of time, it was that the Son of God was going to be crucified. Indeed, Jesus himself had been teaching this very truth to his disciples (Matt. 12:40; 16:21; John 2:19). This makes it all the more amazing that Jesus makes one last attempt to change his Father's plan "if it is possible."

The prayer reveals that in the mind of Jesus there was at least a theoretical chance that another course of action could be taken "at the eleventh hour." It was not possible, of course, so Jesus was crucified. Yet this doesn't negate the fact that Jesus' prayer presupposes that divine plans and possible future events are, in principle, alterable. In short, Jesus' prayer evidences the truth that the future is at least partly open, even if his own fate was not.

Hastening the Lord's Return

Closely related to the conditional way the Lord some-times speaks about the future in Scripture is the flexible way inspired biblical authors describe the future. This con-stitutes the seventh aspect of the motif of future openness we need to discuss.

For example, Peter addresses a group of Christians who are discouraged that the Lord's promised return has been taking so long. He tells them that the Lord has delayed his coming because he is "patient with you, not wanting any to perish" (2 Peter 3:9). He then encourages them to be "waiting for and hastening the coming of the day of God" (3:12) ["speed its coming," NIV].

If taken at face value, the verse is teaching us that how people respond to the gospel and how Christians live affects the timing of the second coming. But how is this teaching compatible with the view that everything, including the timing of the second coming, is eternally fixed in God's mind? What is the point of talking about God's delay due to his patience or encouraging believers to speed up Christ's return by how they live if in reality the exact time has been settled from all eternity?

The "Day and Hour" of the Coming

Part of the reason believers have generally assumed that the timing of the second coming is settled is that Jesus told us that "about that day or hour no one knows, neither the angels in heaven, nor the Son, but only the Father" (Mark 13:32). The meaning of this statement must be considered in relation to 2 Peter 3:9–12. In other words, we cannot simply decide to believe one passage and ignore the other.

As it turns out, there is no difficulty in affirming both texts. Jesus' statement can easily be understood as an idiomatic way of saying that *it lies in the Father's authority,* no one else's, to finally decide when the second coming will occur. It need not mean that the Father has *already set* the exact date.

For example, I may respond to my daughter's question about when she will be old enough to date boys by saying, "I alone know when it's time." But this doesn't mean that the exact date is already fixed in my mind. It simply means that it's in my authority to determine this. I know the kind of maturity I'm looking for to tell me that she's ready to start dating, though I am not certain as to exactly how long it will take for her to acquire this.

Indeed, to press the analogy a bit further, I may actually encourage her to "hasten the day" by acting in a certain manner. So too, we can readily understand how the Lord could tell us that the Father alone "knows about that day or hour" of his return while also, through Peter, encouraging us to speed it up.

Why Create Condemned People?

Another aspect of this passage is worth mentioning. Peter tells us that the delay in Christ's return is due to the fact that God doesn't want "any to perish, but all to come to repentance" (3:9). God wants everyone he's created to turn to him. If everything about the future was settled before God ever created the world, however, God would of course have known exactly who would and would not respond to him. This not only creates difficulties understanding the meaning of God patiently delaying his return as he holds out hope for others to repent, it also raises the even more poignant question as to why God would create people he is certain will go to hell in the first place.

It is not difficult to understand why God sorrowfully allows people to choose evil and hell *once he creates them*. To take back freedom *once it is given* on the grounds that it is being used wrongly would mean that freedom was never given in the first place. This risk is inherent in creating free beings. But it is very difficult to understand why God gives freedom to beings he is certain are going to misuse it to the point of damning themselves to eternal hell. If it is better to never have been born than to suffer in hell, as Jesus says (Matt. 26:24), and if God always does the best thing, why would he not simply refrain from creating these condemned people?

Even more puzzling is the fact that God continues to strive with these people, *trying to get them to believe*. He is grieved when they resist him (see Isa. 63:10; Eph. 4:30; Acts 7:51; Heb. 3:8, 15; 4:7). Why would God expend this energy and experience this frustration if it was from all eternity a foregone conclusion that these fated people would *not* yield to his loving influence? Conversely, doesn't the fact that God sincerely tries to get these people to believe imply that it was not certain to God that they would *not* believe when he created them?

Blotting Out from the Book of Life

Similarly, several times in Scripture God warns people that he may blot their names out of the Book of Life (Exod. 32:33; Rev. 3:5; cf. Rev. 22:18). This raises an interesting question: If God foreknew from all eternity that certain names would be "blotted out" of his book, why did he bother to put them there in the first place? If God may indeed "take away [a] . . . person's share in the tree of life and in the holy city" (Rev. 22:19), and God knew this would happen, why did he give them a share in the first place? If we take these verses at face value, doesn't this "blotting out" and "taking away" describe a genuine change in God's attitude toward these people? And doesn't this change entail that the eternal destiny of these people was not fixed in God's mind from the start?

As the texts stand, they give us every reason to believe that God truly planned on saving these people, which is why their names were written in the book and they were given "a share" of the Tree of Life. Then they rebelled, so his plan for them was altered. They were "blotted out" and their share "taken away." If these texts don't teach us this much, it is not at all clear what they are intended to teach.

From an open view perspective, God creates the people he creates because he sees the possibility (but not the certainty) that they will become citizens of the eternal kingdom. He genuinely strives to win everyone because he hopes that they will surrender to him. When they meet the condition of salvation by exercising faith in him, he writes them in his book. When the condition is lost, so are they.

The God who loves the entire world (John 3:16) is genuinely grieved when this happens. He knows that their loss was not inevitable. They could have, should have, and would have been his children.

So far as I can see, the open view makes better sense out of this wealth of biblical references than the view that people's destinies are certain before they are ever born.

Jeremiah 18 and the Flexible Potter

The final aspect of the motif of future openness we need to examine is also the strongest. Numerous times in Scripture we find that God changes his mind in response to events that transpire in history. By definition, one cannot change what is permanently fixed. Hence, every time the Bible teaches us that God changes his mind it is teaching us that God's mind is not permanently fixed. This directly contradicts the classical understanding of foreknowledge. It means that some of what God knows regarding the future consists of things that *may* go one way or another. He adjusts his plans—changes his mind—depending on what does or does not take place.

This is not merely a logical deduction I am making. It is the explicit teaching of Scripture. Perhaps the best example of this is found in Jeremiah 18. Many in Israel had heard that the Lord was planning on punishing her for her wickedness and had wrongly assumed that this meant "It is no use!" (Jer. 18:12). If God has prophesied against us, they reasoned, there is nothing that can be done about it. It seems that they were reading into God's prophecy the assumption that the future was unalterable.

To correct this fatalistic thinking, the Lord directed Jeremiah to go to a potter's house to watch a potter at work. "The vessel he was making of clay was spoiled in the potter's hand, and he reworked it into another vessel, as seemed good to him" (v. 4). The Lord then instructed Jeremiah: "Can I not do with you, O house of Israel, just as this potter has done? . . . Just like the clay in the potter's hand, so are you in my hand, O house of Israel" (v. 6).

The Lord then continues:

> At one moment I may declare concerning a nation or a kingdom, that I will pluck up and break down and destroy it, but if that nation, concerning which I have spoken, turns from its evil, I will *change my mind* about the disaster that I intended to bring on it. And at another moment I may declare concerning a nation or a kingdom that I will build and plant it, but if it does evil in my sight, not listening to my voice, then I will *change my mind* about the good that I had intended to do to it (vv. 7–10).

The Lord then applies this teaching to Israel: "Look, I am a potter shaping evil against you and devising a plan against you. Turn now, all of you from your evil way, and amend your ways and your doings" (v. 11). There are several points worth making regarding this remarkable passage.

A Virtuously Flexible Omnipotence

First, many ancient and contemporary interpreters have used the potter/clay analogy to argue that God exercises unilateral control over us. They mistakenly read Paul to be using the analogy in this fashion (Rom. 9:21–23). Entering into a full discussion of Paul's analogy would take us too far astray (see chapter 4, question 13). What is important for us to note is that in Jeremiah (the passage Paul is alluding to), the analogy is used to make the *exact opposite point*. As the potter was willing to revise his vessel once the first plan was "spoiled," so God is willing to revise his initial plan when circumstances call for it. He is not a unilaterally controlling God; he is a graciously flexible God. The "clay" he works with is not lifeless but has a mind and will of its own, to which he responds appropriately.

Change and Certainty

Second, we must take very seriously the Lord's word in Jeremiah 18 that he will "change [his] mind about the disaster that [he] intended to bring" on one nation (v. 8) and/or "change [his] mind about the good [he] had intended to do to" another nation, if these nations change (v. 10). If the future were exhaustively fixed, could the Lord genuinely intend to bring something about and then genuinely *change his mind* and not bring it about? How can someone sincerely intend to do something they are certain they will never do? And how can they truly change their mind if their mind is eternally made up?

Is the "Change" Merely Appearance?

Classical theologians usually argue that texts that attribute change to God describe how he *appears* to us; they do not depict God as he really is. It *looks* like God changed his mind, but he *really* didn't.

Unfortunately for the classical interpretation, the text does not say, or remotely imply, that it *looks* like the Lord intended something and then changed his mind. Rather, the Lord himself tells us in the plainest terms possible that he intended one thing and then changed his mind and did something else. How can God's stated intention be explained as an appearance? There is simply no reason to interpret language about changeable aspects of God less literally than language about unchangeable aspects of God.

Suppose, for the sake of argument, that God wanted to tell us in Scripture that he *really does* sometimes intend to carry out one course of action and that he *really does* some-times change his mind and not do it. How could he tell us this in terms clearer than he did in this passage? He says here (and many other places), "I change my mind." How could he say it any clearer? If this passage doesn't teach us that God can truly change his intentions, what would a passage that *did* teach this look like?

I suggest that if this text isn't enough to convince us that God's mind is not eternally settled, then our philosophical presuppositions are controlling our exegesis to a degree that no text could *ever* teach us this. People who affirm the divine authority of Scripture do not want to be guilty of this charge.

The Virtue of Changeability

Fourth, while classical theologians have always considered the notion that God changes his mind as denoting a weakness on God's part, this passage and several others (Jonah 4:2; Joel 2:12–13) consider God's willingness to change to be one of God's attributes of greatness. When a person is in a genuine relationship with another, willingness to adjust to them is always considered a virtue. Why should this apply to people but not to God?

On the contrary, since God is the epitome of everything we deem praiseworthy, and since we ordinarily consider responsiveness to be praiseworthy, should we not be inclined to view God as the *most* responsive being imaginable? He never changes his perfect character, of course, for this would not be praiseworthy. But as Scripture indicates, he is wonderfully willing and able to adjust his plans and emotions as his relationship with us calls for it. The Israelites were mistaken precisely because they didn't appreciate this aspect of God's greatness (Jer. 18:12).

God Is Not a Human That He Should Change

Finally, we must reconcile Jeremiah 18 and all the other passages that speak of God "changing his mind" with Samuel's statement to Saul that "the Glory of Israel will not recant or change his mind; for he is not a mortal, that he should change his mind" (1 Sam. 15:29). A nearly identical statement was made by Balaam when he told Balak, "God is not a human being, that he should lie, or a mortal, that he should change his mind" (Num. 23:19). Some defenders of the classical view of foreknowledge seize these two verses and insist that, unlike all the verses that describe God changing his mind, these *do not* speak figuratively or in terms of how things *appear.* These verses rather describe God as he *really is*—one who does not change his mind.

A closer examination of both passages reveals that they do not contradict the teaching that God changes his mind and do not speak about God any more literally than the passages in which God does change his mind.

God Will Not Change—But He Could

Regarding Samuel's statement to Saul, it is important to recall that both before and after this verse we find Scripture explicitly teaching that God regretted making Saul king over Israel (1 Sam. 15:11, 35). He intended to bless him but ended up judging him instead (1 Sam. 13:13–14). We cannot declare the middle verse to be literal and the other two nonliteral just because the middle verse might fit best with our theological preconceptions. There is no indication in the text of a switch from literal to nonliteral speech.

Some argue that we must consider that some sort of switch occurs, for otherwise we would have to assume that the Bible contradicts itself (in the space of a dozen verses or so!). If we carefully read each verse in context, however, we find that there is no contradiction between them, even if we interpret them all literally.

It's important to note that Samuel had prayed all night trying to change the Lord's mind regarding Saul's dethronement (1 Sam. 15:11–12). This alone is enough to demonstrate that Samuel believed that God could, in principle, change his mind about things. It's just that, after trying all night, he came to conclude that in this instance God *wouldn't* change his mind. There is a big difference between "couldn't" and "wouldn't." The classical view of divine foreknowledge teaches the former, but Scripture on occasion teaches the latter. We find several examples of God declaring, "I *will not* change my mind" (Ezek. 24:14; Zech. 8:14). But note carefully, these exceptions prove the rule. It is only meaningful for God to say he *will not* change his mind if it is true that he *could* change his mind if he wanted to, and if it is true that many times he does want to (see Jer. 18:7–10; Jonah 4:2; Joel 2:12–13).

First Samuel 15:29 does not teach that God couldn't change his mind, only that in this instance he wouldn't change it. Perhaps if Saul had truly repented of his sin instead of begging Samuel to change things with a purely selfish motive (v. 27), God would have reversed his decision once again. Unfortunately, Saul gave God no reason to forgive him or restore him. And, unlike fallible and fickle humans, God can't be cajoled into altering his plans for any reasons other than those that are consistent with his unchanging holy character.

God's Prophecies Are Not for Hire

Something similar may be said regarding Numbers 23:19. In this passage, Balak attempted to get Balaam (a "prophet-for-hire") to prophesy what he wanted to hear (22:38–23:17). The Lord informed Balak that he, the true

God, is not like a human being who can lie when it's profitable or a mortal who will change his mind for the sake of convenience. This was a common practice for false prophets who spoke on behalf of false gods. But for the first time in his life, Balak (and Balaam!) had confronted the real God. This God is not like a mortal who would change his mind for the reasons Balak gave him to do so.

We see that there is no good reason to interpret these two passages more literally than those that teach us God can and does change his mind. If read in context, both sets of verses may be affirmed as accurately depicting God as he really is. God's mind is unchanging in every way that it is virtuous to be unchanging but open to change in every way that it is virtuous to be open. No contradiction needs to be resolved. No strained reinterpretation of a major motif of Scripture is needed. The only thing required is that we accept that the future is partly open as well as partly settled, and thus that God is not only the God of what will certainly be but also the God of all possibilities.

Reversed Divine Intentions

Jeremiah 18 is hardly alone in explicitly declaring the truth that God changes his mind when circumstances call for it. Let us consider several other examples.

Dispatched to Destroy

In 1 Chronicles 21:15, for example, we are told that the Lord, in his righteous anger, "sent an angel to Jerusalem *to destroy it*." However, "when he was about to destroy it, the LORD relented concerning the calamity." We have to wonder: Could the Lord genuinely have intended "to destroy"

Jerusalem—to the point of actually dispatching an angel to accomplish the task—if he was certain from the start that he *wouldn't* destroy the city? If God always knew he wouldn't destroy it, isn't Scripture simply wrong in claiming that God sent the angel "to destroy it"?

Note also how impossible it is to dismiss texts such as this one as speaking only in terms of appearances, not reality. The information that this inspired text imparts to us concerns a subjective motive on God's part that we would not have known about had Scripture not revealed it.

An Expanded Life

Along similar lines, in 2 Kings 20:1–6 the Lord tells Hezekiah through an inspired prophet that he would not recover from his sickness; he would die. Hezekiah pleaded with him, however, and as a result the Lord reversed his stated intention: "I will add fifteen years to your life" (v. 6). Jeremiah later encouraged the fatalistic Israelites by reminding them of this great reversal. "Did [Hezekiah] not fear the Lord and entreat the favor of the Lord, and did not the Lord *change his mind* about the disaster that he had pronounced?" (Jer. 26:19).

Now, if we accept the classical view of foreknowledge and suppose that the Lord was certain that he would *not* let Hezekiah die, wasn't he being duplicitous when he initially told Hezekiah that he would not recover? And if we suppose that the Lord was certain all along that Hezekiah would, in fact, live fifteen years after this episode, wasn't it misleading for God to tell him that he was *adding* fifteen years to his life? Wouldn't Jeremiah also be mistaken in announcing that God *changed his mind* when he reversed his stated intentions to Hezekiah—if, in fact, God's mind never really changes?

Further Examples of Divine Mind Changes

This theme is far more pervasive in Scripture than most believers realize. Consider briefly the following small sampling.

Exodus 32:14. Because of Moses' intercessory prayer, "the LORD *changed his mind* about the disaster that *he planned* to bring on his people." David later recounts this episode when he notes that the Lord "said he would destroy them—had not Moses, his chosen one, stood in the breach before him, to turn away his wrath from destroying them" (Psalm 106:23). Did God really plan on destroying Israel, and did he really change his mind?

Exodus 33:1–3, 14. In the light of Moses' pleading, the Lord reversed his plan not to go with the Israelites into Egypt. Was God simply toying with Moses when he told them he was planning on *not* going?

Deuteronomy 9:13–29. The Lord "*intended* to destroy" the Israelites (v. 25), and was even "ready to destroy" Aaron (v. 20). Moses' forty-day intercession altered God's intention (vv. 25–29). Is Scripture speaking truly when it tells us God intended to do something he later decided not to do? Could God truly intend to do something he was eternally certain he wouldn't do?

1 Samuel 2:27–31. Because Eli "scorned" God's sacrifices and did not punish his sons for their vile behavior, the Lord says, "'I promised that your house and your father's house would minister before me forever.' *But now* the LORD declares: 'Far be it from me! Those who honor me I will honor, but those who despise me will be disdained. The time is coming when I will cut short your strength and the strength of your father's house'" (vv. 30–31 NIV). Could God have authentically promised Eli something he eternally knew would never take place?

1 Kings 21:21–29. The Lord tells Ahab, "I will bring disaster on you" because of his sin (v. 21). Ahab humbles himself before God, and the Lord responds: "Because he has humbled himself before me, I will not bring the disaster in his days" (v. 29). Is not the easiest reading of texts such as these one that simply admits that God truly intended to bring disaster and then changed his mind in response to human repentance?

2 Chronicles 12:5–8. The Lord was going to allow the Israelites to be conquered because of King Rehoboam's rebellion. "You abandoned me, so I have abandoned you to the hand of Shishak" (v. 5). The king and his officers repent, so the Lord changes his plan. "They have humbled themselves; I will not destroy them . . . my wrath shall not be poured out on Jerusalem by the hand of Shishak" (v. 7). Could God really intend to deliver the Israelites over to Shishak if he was eternally certain he wouldn't?

Jeremiah 26:2–3. The Lord tells Jeremiah to prophesy to Israel that they should repent, saying, "I may *change my mind* about the disaster that *I intend* to bring on [Israel] because of their evil doings" (v. 3). If in truth God never changes his mind, is he not lying when he tells the Israelites that he might do so? Is there not something odd going on in evangelicalism today when certain believers (open theists) are labeled heretical for taking God's promise ("I may change my mind") literally? Indeed, isn't the point of this and similar passages (see Jer. 18:7–10; 26:19; Joel 2:12–13; Jonah 4:2) precisely to *encourage* people to think about God as one who really is willing to change his mind? Can anyone be faulted for taking this encouragement to heart?

Ezekiel 4:9–15. As an object lesson, the Lord tells Ezekiel to cook some food using human excrement as fuel (vv. 12–13). Ezekiel finds this too offensive and objects. So the Lord says, "I will let you use cow's dung instead of human dung" (v. 15). The passage reveals God's willingness to adjust his plans in response to the sentiments of his children. What was the point of God's first command if he was certain he would revise it in the light of Ezekiel's objection?

Amos 7:1–6. The Lord revealed two judgments he was planning on bringing upon Israel. Twice Amos intercedes, and twice Scripture says, "The LORD *relented* concerning this . . ." (vv. 3, 6). Was the Lord simply toying with Amos when he showed him what he planned on doing to Israel? Is there any other way to view God's interaction with Amos if we believe that God was certain all along that he wasn't going to bring these visions about?

Jonah 3:10. God *"changed his mind"* about the destruction he planned to carry out on Nineveh. Note, neither this nor any other verse says or even remotely suggests that God *appeared* to change his mind. It simply says, in as plain and straightforward a way as can be imagined, that God "changed his mind."

The list could be expanded, but the point has been made (see the appendix for further examples). Clearly, the motif that God changes his mind is not an incidental one in Scripture. It runs throughout the biblical narrative and is even exalted as one of his praiseworthy attributes. It is very difficult to see how passages such as these can be fairly interpreted if we assume that the future is exhaustively settled and known by God as such.

If we simply free ourselves from the Hellenistic philosophical assumptions that God must be unchanging *in every respect* and that time is an illusion, we will be able to embrace the plain meaning of these texts along with the glorious picture of divine sovereignty and openness that they engender. God is not only the God of future certainties; he's the God of future possibilities.

Conclusion

In this chapter, we have examined the scriptural themes that together constitute the biblical motif of future openness. These passages suggest that the future is partly open just as clearly as the passages that constitute the motif of future determinism depict the future as partly settled. Put together, and taken at their face value, these two motifs lead us to the simple conclusion that the future is partly open and partly settled.

Classical theology cannot accept this conclusion because of philosophical preconceptions of what God must be like: He must be in every respect unchanging, so his knowledge of the future must be unchanging. This is why those holding this view were forced to reinterpret the motif of future openness in strained ways, as we have seen.

Because of this philosophical presupposition, God is not allowed to say what he wants to say in Scripture. Suppose, for the sake of argument, that God wanted to tell us he really *does* change his mind. How could he do so in terms clearer than he did in passages such as Jeremiah 18:8 and 10 in which he explicitly tells us, "I will change my mind"? Or suppose, for the sake of argument, that God wanted to tell us he really *does* regret certain decisions he's made and really *does* experience unexpected disappointment. How could he do so in terms clearer than he did in passages such as 1 Samuel 15:11 in which he explicitly tells us, "I regret that I made Saul king," or Jeremiah 3:7 in which he tells us, "I thought . . . 'she will return to me'; but she did not return"? It's difficult to conceive of how God could be more explicit. The fact that verses as explicit as these aren't allowed to communicate that God really changes his mind or experiences regret or unexpected disappointment testifies to the truth that the classical exegesis of these passages is driven by philosophy rather than by the texts. If these verses aren't allowed to teach these truths, no verse ever could. In short, it seems that what Scripture is allowed to teach about God has been decided ahead of time—on the basis of a philosophical preconception of what God must be like.

On the other hand, if we simply accept the plain meaning of Scripture, we learn that God sometimes regrets how decisions he's made turn out. He sometimes questions how aspects of the future will go. Other times he confronts the unexpected and experiences frustration because free agents choose unlikely courses of action. We learn that many times God tests his children "to know" their character, which is being formed by their decisions. Often God speaks and thinks in terms of what may or may not occur. And, we have seen, many times he genuinely changes his mind about intended courses of action.

If we do not read into this material a philosophical preconception about what God must be like, we have no problem affirming this motif of future openness alongside the motif of future determinism. Indeed, the two motifs are complimentary and together constitute the one perspective that squares with our actual experience of the world. As noted in the previous chapter, with every decision we make we assume that the future is partly open and partly settled.

This concludes our investigation of the biblical side of the open theism debate. Two more tasks remain to be accomplished, however. First, since the pragmatic viability of a theory is one test of its truthfulness, we must flesh out some of the practical implications of the open view. This will be our goal in the next chapter. Second, since the ability of a theory to answer difficult objections is another test of its truthfulness, I will respond to the most common philosophical and theological objections to the open view in the fourth and final chapter of this work.

THREE

What Practical Difference Does the Open View Make?

"So what?" the reader may be asking. "What difference does it really make whether you believe that the future is exhaustively settled or only partially settled? This seems to be a minor point in the total scheme of things."

My first reaction is to agree. In the light of all that Christians share in Christ, the disagreement between the open view of God and the future and the classical view is minor. Over and against all who refuse to bow their knee to the Lord, we are in truth a newly created humanity (Eph.

2:14–16), and *all* of our differences, doctrinal and otherwise, become minor in light of this. It is crucial to the health of the church that we regularly celebrate this unity.

It is also important, however, that we learn from each other by openly and lovingly discussing our differences amidst our unity. This is not only an intellectual exercise; the beliefs we hold make a practical difference in our lives. Indeed, one of the things we need to discuss is how the various opinions we hold might affect our lives in different ways. This is what I'd like to do in this chapter. Having presented the biblical reasons why a person might embrace the open view of God and the future, I'd like to highlight seven areas in which I believe this view might positively affect the quality of our faith and lives.

Rational Minds and Transformed Hearts

Though some people are clearly more intellectually driven than others, all of us are created to have our minds and our hearts work in sync with each other. Striving to have a plausible theology is necessary because, for many of us, the mind must be thoroughly convinced if the heart is to be thoroughly transformed.

Though I lovingly acknowledge that many will disagree with me on this point, I would argue that the open view of God and of the future makes more intellectual sense than the classical view. As a result, many have found this view to have a transforming, passion-infusing effect on their lives once they have embraced it.

It is the only view that allows us to affirm that the way things *appear* is basically the way things actually *are*. As noted in chapter 2, the open view is also the only view that reflects the way we actually live. With every decision, we reveal the fundamental assumption that the future is partly open and is in part up to us to create. The open view is the only option that avoids the impenetrable paradox (or, many of us would argue, the contradiction) of asserting that self-determining free actions are settled an eternity before free agents make them so.

The incongruity between the classical view of fore-knowledge and our experience, together with the difficult paradox it requires us to accept, gives a sense of unreality to the classical view, at least for some people. Whether they are aware of it or not, this sense of unreality can adversely affect the passion with which these people embrace and live out their faith. The open view, by contrast, has for many the "ring of truth" precisely because it is consistent with the way we experience the world and the way we experience ourselves as decision-making beings. And it doesn't require accepting the impenetrable paradox that our decisions are settled an eternity before we create them. For these reasons, I would suggest that the open view is more relevant to our lives than the classical view.

The Clarity of God's Word

Second, one of the most important considerations in assessing the plausibility of any theological position is whether it is able to reconcile coherently elements of God's Word that otherwise stand in tension with each other. The doctrine of the Trinity, for example, was deemed plausible by the early church largely on the grounds that it was able to reconcile the otherwise disparate teachings that there is only one God and yet that the Father, Son, and Holy Spirit are each fully God. So too, the doctrine of the incarnation was deemed plausible by the early church largely on the grounds that it was able to reconcile the seemingly contradictory teachings that Jesus is fully human, on the one hand, and the teaching that he is fully God, on the other.

Such doctrines provide a framework in which the Word of God *makes sense,* and this, as was suggested above, is important for the Word of God to have as much impact on our lives as possible. By bringing coherence to the Word, such beliefs unlock the door that allows us to enter into the truth of Scripture with confidence and be transformed by this truth. The extent to which the Word of God is incoherent to us is the extent to which it is of no benefit to us.

Though the open view is not on the same level as the doctrines of the Trinity and the incarnation, I believe that it also reconciles other seemingly contradictory passages of the Word. It provides us with a framework in which the Word in its entirety begins to make sense on this issue. The teachings regarding God's settled foreknowledge and God's openness to future possibilities are brought together into a coherent framework. The removal of this subtle incoherence increases our ability to understand God more clearly, relate to him more sincerely, and be transformed by him more profoundly.

The God of the Possible and Possibility Living

Your Picture of God

Third, the openness issue affects a person's view of God in significant ways. A person's mental picture of God is the most important feature of his or her belief system. This picture determines how we relate to God, for better or for worse. Most of the time we are unaware of our deepest beliefs about God. We may *think* we believe one thing about God, repeating teachings we have been given, when in fact, at a deeper level, our picture of God does not actually reflect these teachings. And since our hearts always respond to what we *really* believe, not what we *think* we believe on a theoretical level, our lives frequently don't reflect what we say we believe.

For example, if asked what we believe God is like, we may be conditioned to repeat the phrase, "God is love." Yet we may not feel loved and thus may not be in the process of being transformed by God's love. The picture of God we *really* hold has been derived (perhaps) from our unloving earthly father or from negative life experiences instead of from the Bible, centered on the person of Jesus Christ.

Revolt versus Resignation

How does all this relate to the open view of God? I believe that in a subtle way the doctrine that the future is eternally settled in the mind of God sometimes contributes to a harmful picture of God. Because this picture holds that God experiences no possibilities, it indirectly suggests that possibilities are not real, for God's knowledge, not ours, reflects reality *as it really is.* If we believe that possibilities are not real, we will be more inclined to accept things that we could, and *should,* revolt against.

For example, despite our talk to the contrary, and despite the fact that life forces us to decide between possibilities, many Christians reflect an attitude of resignation toward sin and evil in their own lives and in the world around them. They do not strive for the possibility of change in their lives and in the world as passionately as they could. At a certain level, I believe that the assumption that the future is in every respect settled contributes to this.

Conversely, if we believe in the reality of possibilities, for even God faces them, we will be more inclined to take a proactive stance. Knowing that what transpires in the future is not a foregone conclusion but is significantly up to us to decide, we will be more inclined to assume responsibility for our future. What we *really* believe—at a level that is more fundamental than words—influences how we behave.

The Positive Nature of Possibilities

Along the same lines, if we believe that even God faces possibilities, we will be more inclined to see possibilities as positive than if we believe God faces an exhaustively settled future. In contrast to the classical perspective, the open view sees possibilities as more than the by-product of our limited human perspective. Possibilities are a crucial aspect of reality, even for God. People who believe this will be more inclined to think of their lives in terms of possibilities. They will be more inclined to adventurously and passionately envisage and pursue what they *could* be instead of resigning themselves to what was supposedly settled an eternity ago about what they *will* be.

The bottom line is that *life is all about possibilities*. We are thinking, feeling, willing, personal beings only because we, like God, are beings who can reflect on and choose between possibilities. We are fully alive when we passionately seize them, adventurously explore them, and define ourselves by actualizing them. Any picture of God that suggests, however indirectly, that possibilities are not ultimately real subtly undermines the passion of those who embrace this belief at a core level. Conversely, the picture of God as the "God of the possible" creates a people who do not wait for an eternally settled future to happen. Through God's grace and power, they help *create* the future.

The Urgency of Prayer

The Problem of Prayer

Our fourth practical point builds on the insight stated earlier that our hearts respond to things more passionately if our minds are able to understand them. My conviction is that many Christians do not pray as passionately as they could because they don't see how it could make any significant difference. They pray, but they often do so out of sheer obedience and without the sense of urgency that Scripture consistently attaches to prayer.

The problem, I believe, is that despite all the pious talk about how God wants and even needs us to pray, many Christians have an understanding of divine sovereignty in which the urgency of prayer simply doesn't make much sense. Regardless of what Scripture teaches (e.g., Jer. 18:7–11), they believe that God's plans cannot *truly* be changed; the future is exhaustively settled. They interpret the cliché "God is in control" to mean that "God controls everything." So the obvious question is, What *real* difference could prayer possibly make? The common saying that "prayer changes us, not God" simply doesn't reflect the purpose or the urgency that Scripture gives to petitionary prayer.

Because it holds that the future is *not* entirely settled and that God's plans *can* change, the open view is able to render the purpose and urgency of prayer intelligible in a way that neither classical Arminianism nor classical Calvinism can. The open view is able to declare, without qualification or inconsistency, that some of the future *genuinely depends on prayer*. On a practical level, this translates into people who are more inclined to pray with passion and urgency.

Exercising Spiritual "Say-So"

To flesh out the matter a bit further, the open view holds that because God's goal of creation is the participation of humans (and in some sense, angels) in the loving triune relationship that God is throughout eternity, he wanted a creation that consisted of personal, morally responsible, free agents. He thus ordained that we have "say-so" in how things transpire. He doesn't want to relate to robots; he wants to interact with real persons. There can be no authentic personhood without some element of say-so, some degree of self-determination, some authentic power to influence things.

Most believers recognize that we have been given such say-so on a physical level. We instinctively know that our future as well as the future of our children, our spouse, our neighbors, and others is significantly influenced by what we think, say, and do. Say-so on this level is what makes us morally responsible agents. What is usually not so evident, however, is that we have this same sort of say-so on a spiritual level as well. Prayer is also part of what makes us morally responsible agents.

Because God wants us to be empowered, because he desires us to communicate with him, and because he wants us to learn dependency on him, he graciously grants us the ability to significantly affect him. This is the power of petitionary prayer. God displays his beautiful sovereignty by deciding *not* to always unilaterally decide matters. He enlists our input, not because he needs it, but because he desires to have an authentic, dynamic relationship with us as real, empowered persons. Like a loving parent or spouse, he wants not only to influence us but to be influenced *by us*.

Jesus drives home this point with his parable of a widow who persistently bothered an unjust judge until he granted her justice, just so she would leave him alone (Luke 18:2–5). The parable teaches us about our "need to pray always and not lose heart" (v. 1). If even an unjust judge will relent and hear a widow's persistent plea, Jesus is saying, how much more will our loving Father be affected by our persistent pleas?

In the open view, God has sovereignly ordained that prayer be one of our central means of influencing what transpires in history. It is our means of influencing God's decisions about the future—sometimes, Scripture indicates, to the point that he reverses his own plans, as we saw in chapter 2. God binds himself to this arrangement, even abandoning plans he'd rather carry out because people didn't pray, as we also saw in chapter 2. The Lord does not play with words when he teaches and illustrates throughout Scripture that much of what will happen in the future depends on prayer: "*If* my people . . . humble themselves [and] pray . . . *then* will I hear from heaven . . . and heal their land" (2 Chron. 7:14).

"Say-So" and Moral Responsibility

Though this is simplistic, it might help if we think of God's power and our say-so in terms of percentages. Prior to creation, God possessed 100 percent of all power. He possessed all the say-so there was. When the Trinity decided to express their love by bringing forth a creation, they invested each creature (angelic and human) with a certain percentage of their say-so. The say-so of the triune God was at this point no longer the only one that determined how things would go. God's personal creations now possessed a measure of ability to influence what would occur. This was necessary (as was the risk that went with it) if God's creations were to be personal beings who had the ability to make authentic choices, including the choice whether to enter into a loving relationship with him.

In the case of humans at least (angels are another story), our say-so is designed to be spent on both a physical and spiritual plane. We can choose to either work with or against God in terms of how we live and affect other people physically. We can also choose either to work for or against God spiritually by "cashing in" on our say-so, as it were, utilizing the power of prayer that he has ordained for us. We are morally responsible for how we use or don't use both, for aspects of the future truly depend on us.

I do not see that any view of God captures the power and urgency of prayer as adequately as the open view does, and, because the heart is influenced by the mind, I do not see that any view can inspire passionate and urgent prayer as powerfully as the open view.

Resolving the Problem of Evil

The fifth practical difference that the open view makes concerns our understanding and response to the problem of evil.

Foreknowing and Allowing Atrocities

A number of years ago, my agnostic father and I were conversing by letter about the problem of how an all-good, all-powerful God could allow nightmarish suffering to occur in his creation. In one correspondence, my father asked me why God would allow Adolf Hitler to be born if he foreknew that this man would massacre millions of Jews. It was a very good question. The only response I could offer then, and the only response I continue to offer now, is that this was not foreknown as a certainty at the time God created Hitler.[1]

If you claim that God foreknew exactly what Hitler would do and created him anyway, it's hard to avoid the conclusion that the world must somehow be better with Hitler than without him. Think about it. If God is all good and thus always does what is best, and if God knew exactly what Hitler would do when he created him, we must conclude that God believed that allowing Hitler's massacre of the Jews (and many others) was preferable to his not allowing it. If you accept the premises that God is all good and all powerful and that he possesses exhaustively settled foreknowledge, the conclusion is difficult to avoid.

There's a Purpose for Everything?

For the most part, the classical theology of the church has not shied away from this conclusion. Though classical theologians have proposed a number of different reasons why God allows suffering, they have tended to agree that there is a specific divine purpose for every specific event, including specific evils. It is *this* conclusion more than anything else that creates the problem of evil, for it immediately leads to the impervious mystery of what purpose an all-loving God might have had for allowing atrocities such as the Holocaust.

I do not want to claim that the open view entirely solves the problem of evil. Much more needs to be said about this matter than can be said at present. But I believe it offers the most plausible way out of the dilemma of assuming God has a purpose for allowing particular evils. True, God must have a purpose for giving free agents the *potential* to make evil choices. In my view, he could not give them the potential to choose love without also giving them the potential to choose against it. Hence, the potential for evil lies in the nature of free will (see chapter 4, question 9). Once God gave people this freedom, however, the purpose for their actions lies in *them*, not God. Since it was not settled ahead of time how people would use the freedom God gave them, God cannot be blamed for how they use it.[2]

Creating Damned Individuals

The problem the classical view of foreknowledge faces regarding evil is particularly intense when we consider hell. If it is difficult to suppose that God allows all temporal suffering because he foresees a higher purpose behind it, how much more difficult is it to suppose that God has a higher purpose for creating individuals he is certain will be damned to eternal suffering in hell? If God eternally foreknew that certain individuals would end up damning themselves, and if, as the Bible says, God takes no delight in the destruction of the wicked but wants everyone to be saved (Ezek. 18:23; 1 Tim. 2:3–4; 2 Peter 3:9), why would he go ahead and create such individuals?

Some might respond by arguing that it is just as difficult to explain why God would allow people to go to hell *after* he created them, as the open view holds, as it is to explain why he would create people he foreknew would go to hell, as the classical view holds. However, there is a world of difference between creating a person with the *possibility* of going to hell and creating a person with the *certainty* of going to hell. If God creates people with the possibility of going to hell, he is not responsible if they choose to actualize this possibility. He allows them to go to hell because not allowing them to do so would render their freedom to reject God's gracious offer of eternal life disingenuous. This explanation is not open to someone who holds that the destiny of people is settled before they are ever created.

Things become even more questionable for the classical view if we consider that according to Scripture, God not only creates damned individuals but strives to bring them into heaven as well. Scripture depicts God as genuinely frustrated and grieved when people resist the Holy Spirit's influence in their lives (Isa. 63:10; Eph. 4:30). Such striving and grief make perfect sense if God knew it was *possible* and *hoped* that these individuals would accept his love, but it is inexplicable if the fate of these individuals was certain to God before he created them. In this view, it was never really possible for these people to accept God and thus there was nothing for God to hope for. How are we to conceive of the all-wise Creator striving for something he eternally knew could never be and being frustrated about something he eternally knew would always be?

Cassandra-Type Foreknowledge

A few theologians have circumvented this problem by revising the classical view of divine foreknowledge slightly. They suggest that God foreknows what will occur but can do nothing about it. The view is called "simple foreknowledge," for God "simply" foreknows what will take place but cannot alter it. In this view, then, God foreknows that certain individuals will go to hell and knows that certain individuals will carry out atrocities, but he is not free to alter these future facts.

This view avoids the problem of evil better than the more traditional view of foreknowledge, but it has problems of its own. For one thing, this view puts God in the same helpless position as the prophetess Cassandra found in Greek mythology. This unfortunate woman was cursed with the ability to foresee disaster while being unable to do anything about it. The difference is that with God, the situation is even more tragic, for in this view God has to helplessly anticipate all the horrors of world history for an eternity!

This view is inconsistent with the Bible's teaching about God's foreknowledge, for as we have seen (chapter 1), whenever the Bible speaks of God's foreknowledge, it is to emphasize his ability to control what comes to pass, not to declare that he knows a future he can't control. The view is inconsistent with the biblical portrayal of the Creator's power over his creation as well. All Bible-believing Christians agree that God created the world freely and is able to intervene in miraculous ways. If we admit that God freely chose to create the world, however, how could we possibly hold that he was not free to choose to create or refrain from creating any particular individual in the world? If we also admit that God is able to intervene miraculously to alter things throughout the course of history, how can we possibly hold that he is not free to intervene to alter things from the moment he first knows they will occur—from eternity?

I do not see how the concept of "simple foreknowledge" could have a good response to these questions. I do not see how the classical view of foreknowledge can be embraced without accepting the difficult conclusion that the horrors of world history and the eternal torment of the damned somehow make a positive contribution to God's creation.

An Activist's Faith

This leads to our final practical implication of the open view as it concerns evil. When we rid ourselves of any lingering suspicion that evil somehow fits into the eternal purposes of God, we are more inclined to be motivated to do something about it. Jesus spent his entire ministry revolting against the evil he confronted. He never suggested that any of the physical or spiritual afflictions he confronted somehow fit into his Father's plan. Rather, he confronted these things as coming from the devil and carried out the Father's plan by healing people and delivering them.[3] We who are Christ's disciples are called to follow our master's lead. We are to pray that the Father's will *would be done* (Matt. 6:10), not accept things as though his will was *already being done!*

The open view, I submit, allows us to say consistently in unequivocal terms that the ultimate source for all evil is found in the will of free agents rather than in God. It thereby renders intelligible God's radical opposition to all forms of evil. Thus it motivates us to rise up aggressively against all evil with the mighty kingdom power of God's Spirit that he has placed in us.

Resolving Difficult Issues in Life

The sixth practical area in which the open view of the future makes a difference concerns our approach to understanding certain troublesome situations. The best way I can make my point is by giving a real-life illustration.

Several years ago after preaching a sermon on how God directs our paths, I was approached by an angry young woman (I'll call her Suzanne). Once I was able to get past the initial raging words—directed more against God than they were against me—Suzanne told me her tragic story.

Suzanne had been raised in a wonderful Christian home and had from a very young age been a passionate, godly disciple of Jesus Christ. Indeed, since her early teen years, her only aspirations in life were to be a missionary to Taiwan and to marry a godly man with a similar vision with whom she could raise a godly, missionary-minded family. She had accepted the common evangelical myth that God had one right man picked out for her and so had committed herself to praying daily for this future husband. She prayed that he would acquire a similar vision to evangelize Taiwan, that he would remain faithful to the Lord and remain pure in heart, and so on.

Suzanne eventually went to a Christian college and, quite miraculously, quickly met a young man who shared her vision for Taiwan. Indeed, the commonalities between them as well as all the "coincidences" that had individually led them to just that college at just that time were truly astounding. For three and a half years they courted one another, prayed together, attended church together, prepared themselves for the mission field, and fell deeply in love with one another. During their senior year, this man proposed to Suzanne; surprisingly, she did not immediately say yes to his proposal. Even though so many pieces had miraculously fallen into place, she needed to have an unequivocal confirmation in her heart that this was the man she was to marry.

For several months, Suzanne and her boyfriend fasted and prayed over the matter. They consulted with their parents, their pastor, and their friends, who agreed to give the matter prayerful attention. Everyone concluded that this marriage was indeed God's will. Before too long, God gave Suzanne the confirmation she needed. While in prayer, she was overwhelmed by a supernatural sense of joy and peace wrapped up with a very clear confirmation that this marriage was, in fact, God's design for her life.

Shortly after college, the newly married couple went away to a missionary school to prepare for their missionary career. Two years into this training, Suzanne learned to her horror that her husband was involved in an adulterous relationship with a fellow student. Her husband repented, but within several months returned to the affair. Despite intensive Christian counseling, this pattern repeated itself several times over the next three years.

During these three years, Suzanne's husband's spiritual convictions altogether disappeared, including his burden for Taiwan. He grew increasingly argumentative, hostile, and even verbally and physically abusive. In one argument toward the end of their marriage, he actually fractured Suzanne's cheekbone in a fit of rage. Soon after this event, Suzanne's husband filed for divorce and moved in with his lover. Two weeks later, Suzanne discovered she was pregnant.

The whole sad ordeal left Suzanne emotionally destroyed and spiritually bankrupt. All of her dreams had crashed down on her. She felt that her life was basically over. The worst part of it, however, was not the pain her husband had inflicted on her. The worst part of it was how profoundly the ordeal had damaged her previously vibrant relationship with the Lord.

Understandably, Suzanne could not fathom how the Lord could respond to her lifelong prayers by setting her up with a man he *knew* would do this to her and her child. Some Christian friends had suggested that perhaps she hadn't heard God correctly. But if it wasn't God's voice that she and everyone else had heard regarding this marriage, she concluded, then no one could ever be sure they heard God's voice. This was as clear as it could ever get. She had a very good point.

Other friends, reminiscent of Job's friends, suggested that her marriage had indeed been God's will. Knowing its outcome, the Lord had led her into it because he loves her so much and was trying to humble her, build her character, or perhaps punish her for previous sin. If a lesson was the point of it all, Suzanne remarked, then God is a very poor teacher. The ordeal didn't teach her anything; it simply left her bitter.

Initially, I tried to help Suzanne understand that this was her ex-husband's fault, not God's, but her reply was more than adequate to invalidate my encouragement: If God *knew* exactly what her husband would do, then he bears all the responsibility for setting her up the way he did. I could not argue against her point, but I could offer an alternative way of understanding the situation.

I suggested to her that God felt as much regret over the confirmation he had given Suzanne as he did about his decision to make Saul king of Israel (1 Sam. 15:11, 35; see also Gen. 6:5–6). Not that it was a bad decision—at the time, her ex-husband was a good man with a godly character. The prospects that he and Suzanne would have a happy marriage and fruitful ministry were, at the time, very good. Indeed, I strongly suspect that he had influenced Suzanne and her ex-husband toward this college with their marriage in mind.

Because her ex-husband was a free agent, however, even the best decisions can have sad results. Over time, and through a series of choices, Suzanne's ex-husband had opened himself up to the enemy's influence and became involved in an immoral relationship. Initially, all was not lost, and God and others tried to restore him, but he chose to resist the prompting of the Spirit, and consequently his heart grew darker. Suzanne's ex-husband had become a very different person from the man God had confirmed to Suzanne to be a good candidate for marriage. This, I assured Suzanne, grieved God's heart at least as deeply as it grieved hers.

By framing the ordeal within the context of an open future, Suzanne was able to understand the tragedy of her life in a new way. She didn't have to abandon all confidence in her ability to hear God and didn't have to accept that somehow God intended this ordeal "for her own good." Her faith in God's character and her love toward God were eventually restored and she was finally able to move on with her life.

Understandably, Taiwan was no longer on her heart, but fortunately, the "God of the possible" always has a plan B and a plan C. He's also wise enough to know how to weave our failed plan A's into these alternative plans so beautifully that looking back, it may look like B or C was his original plan all along. This isn't a testimony to his exhaustive definite foreknowledge; it's a testimony to his unfathomable wisdom.

Without having the open view to offer, I don't know how one could effectively minister to a person in Suzanne's dilemma.

Integration of Theology and Recent Scientific Advances

The seventh and final area in which I believe an open theology can make a practical difference in our lives concerns its ability to interact effectively with many advances in contemporary science. As Christians, we of course want our worldview to be fundamentally derived from God's Word, not the climate of opinion that happens to prevail in the world in which we live. Still, since "all truth is God's truth," as Aquinas taught us, we should assume that whatever is true about the views of our culture, including the views of science, will be consistent with God's Word (assuming we are interpreting it correctly).

Locating this element of truth in the culture and aligning it with our theology based on the Word can be advantageous to communicating credibly the truth of the Word to our culture. It can also help us more effectively think through and apply our theology for our culture and for ourselves. This is why our theology should be developed in dialogue with every other branch of learning. Whatever truth is to be found in physics, cosmology, psychology, sociology, biology, anthropology, and so on is *God's* truth and can only help us credibly proclaim the truth of God's Word to the world.

In this light, it is important to recognize that this century has witnessed a revolution in all of these fields of learning in terms of how we see the world. We have been shifting from a static to a thoroughly dynamic understanding of reality. For example, the Platonic notion that time and change were less real than timeless stability is being abandoned in light of the discovery that many of the world's fundamental processes are unidirectional and irreversible. Increasingly, physicists and others are working on the assumption that time is real.[4] Similarly, the ancient belief that the world is ultimately composed of individual solid things (atoms) has now been completely abandoned because of the discovery in this century that the physical world is rather composed of microscopic dynamic events (quantum energy bursts).

In the same way, the old Newtonian assumption that the world moves forward in a deterministic fashion has been replaced in quantum theory by an understanding of causation that includes an intrinsic element of indeterminism. The previous universally held assumption that science could, in principle, predict everything about the future has (especially among recent chaos theorists) given way to the understanding that an element of unpredictability is intrinsic to significantly complex systems. In short, the old assumption that the world is a stable, solid, deterministic, thoroughly rational, and utterly predictable system has been replaced by a view of the world as a dynamic process that is to some extent indeterministic and unpredictable.

This drastic alteration is not an arbitrary shift of preferences on the part of scientists and philosophers. Indeed, many have strongly resisted it. This shift has occurred because the evidence has forced it. While there are many particular issues that continue to be debated in every branch of modern science, the necessity of this shift toward understanding reality as a dynamic process is no longer in question. It seems as though it is here to stay.

The most fundamental challenge this shift poses for Christian theology is this: The classical view of God and of creation was thoroughly influenced by, and is logically tied to, the old understanding of reality. Hence, the more influential the dynamic understanding of reality becomes in our culture, the more out of sync classical theology will be with our culture.

Now, if classical theology, and thus the old view of the world, was based on the Word of God, we would simply have to say, "Too bad." We would, I suppose, have to conclude that this entire shift is erroneous. But as I have suggested at several points throughout this work, certain aspects of classical theology are not at all required by Scripture. More specifically, the view of God as eternally unchanging in every respect (and thus as possessing an eternal unchanging knowledge of all of world history) owes more to Plato than it does the Bible. It squared with the old worldview because it was itself in large part *the product* of the old worldview.

Therefore, there is no reason for theology to resist the paradigmatic shift occurring in our culture. On the contrary, there are actually good grounds for embracing and celebrating much of it. This shift has to some extent freed us to recognize just how dependent our theology had been on pagan philosophical thought and thus to rediscover the marvelously open and dynamic dimension of God proclaimed in the Word that classical theology had previously minimized.

I would argue that the open view is more consistent with this present shift toward dynamic categories than the classical view that the future is eternally settled in God's mind. The biblical understanding of divine providence and of the future as partly open and partly settled anticipates everything that is being discovered about dynamic systems in various fields of science today.

For example, as previously mentioned, quantum theory tells us that we can predict the range of possible behaviors of a given quantum particle before a quantum measurement, but we cannot predict its exact behavior. Similarly, we can statistically predict very accurately how large groups of quantum particles will behave, but not precisely how any one of them in particular will behave. Quantum mechanics has demonstrated that this uncertainty is not due to our limited measuring devices; it is actually rooted in the nature of things.

This means that even on a quantum level the future is partly open and partly settled. It seems that the balance between openness and settledness permeates reality. The world at every level seems to be constituted as a marvelous dance that exemplifies both form and freedom. There is structure and spontaneity, predictability and unpredictability, everywhere we look.

For example, we can generally predict how large groups of ants will function together but cannot precisely predict what any individual ant will do. We can predict how groups of mammals will behave in certain circumstances but not exactly how any individual within this group will behave. We can predict in general terms when a tornado may form, and we're getting better at this, but we also now know that no amount of information will allow us to specify the exact time and place it will form, and still less how it will behave after it has formed.

We can also discern this balance between openness and settledness in our own lives. Much of what we will do tomorrow is already determined because of our genes, environment, commitments, the character we've acquired thus far, and so on. But at least some of what we will do tomorrow is not settled. We act on the assumption that there is an element of tomorrow that is strictly up to us. Our tomorrow is to some degree open. Nothing will determine every thought we will think or every move we will make. Our lives thus manifest an element of freedom and unpredictability within an overall predictable framework.

The world seems to be exhaustively structured around this intriguing interplay of freedom and determinism, and this is precisely what we would expect if the open view of God and creation is correct. In this view, God's own being exemplifies this interplay. He is determinate and "necessary" in some respects—he cannot fail to be triune or perfectly loving. But he is free in many other respects—whether or not he would choose to express his triune love by creating a world.

His providential involvement in the world exemplifies the same balance. Whatever is necessary to preserve God's plan for creation is predestined, but within this predestined structure there is room for significant freedom. While this strikes some as paradoxical, it is so only within the context of the now-debunked deterministic framework of the past. In actuality, God's ability to move forward in this balance is, in principle, no more paradoxical than our ability to predict, say, the ongoing existence of a leaf, despite the uncertainty that exists in all of the quantum particles that make up a leaf. The structure of the leaf defines the parameters within which the quantum particles must spontaneously act, and the structure of creation and of history, designed by God, sets the parameters within which all human freedom (and all other contingencies) must occur.

In my estimation, this perspective of God and of creation is unparalleled in terms of its wonder, beauty, and explanatory power. God is an eternal triune dance of love who eternally displays structure and freedom. His creation, which he invites to join his dance, manifests the same balance of structure and freedom. The freedom within structure that characterizes our lives manifests it. The ebb and flow of human history manifests it. The insect and animal kingdoms manifest it. Weather patterns and all complex physical processes manifest it. Quantum particles, together with every physical thing that exists, manifest it.

In a word, all reality manifests it. From God to the smallest quantum particle, we find a dance structured by form and exemplifying freedom. Science confirms what the Bible declares: The future is partly open as well as partly settled.

Conclusion

On the basis of the seven points covered in this chapter, I am led to conclude that the belief that the future is to some extent open-ended and that God knows it as such has some important, beneficial, and practical implications for our lives. Since true theories usually work better than false ones, these considerations support the truthfulness of the open view. Add this to the case we have made for the open view throughout this book and you have, I think, some rather compelling reasons for adopting this perspective.

Scripture confirms it with its balance of passages reflecting a partly open future and a partly settled future. Our experience of ourselves confirms it in every self-conscious thought we think and every free decision we make. We live as if the future is partly open. Our experience of the world universally confirms it as we experience structure and freedom all around us—in the children spontaneously playing on the beach, the swarm of gnats dancing like a ball in the air, and the randomly patterned traffic on the freeway. Finally, science confirms it, showing us that every solid thing we behold is simply a patterned statistical regularity composed of a myriad of somewhat spontaneous quantum events.

It's all part of the marvelous dance of God's creation. You can recognize an element of freedom and spontaneity at every level of existence—if you haven't been blinded by a philosophy that tells you it is an illusion.

FOUR

Questions and Objections

We have examined the most significant passages of Scripture that demonstrate that the future is partly settled (chapter 1) as well as those that demonstrate that it is partly open (chapter 2). We have also examined seven areas in which embracing this view of God and the future might have a positive impact on a person's life (chapter 3). On this basis, an increasing number of evangelicals have come to believe that the open view of God and the future is correct.

Though the open view is deeply rooted in Scripture and is pragmatically advantageous, it is admittedly not the traditional perspective. To be sure, it has on occasion been espoused by orthodox Christians going back at least to the fifth century (see question 1), but it has never seriously rivaled the classical view. This justifiably concerns some evangelical Christians. Yet if we affirm that the Bible is our ultimate authority in matters of faith, the nontraditional nature of this view should not automatically rule it out. It should rather lead us to a cautious investigation. If the view is true, it ought to be able to handle the questions and objections raised against it.

This is what I will attempt to do in this chapter. I will consider the eighteen most frequently asked questions and most common objections raised against the open view. My thesis is that the open view is able to adequately answer each of these questions and overcome each objection.

As mentioned in the introduction, the lay reader should be forewarned that a few of these questions are rather philosophical in nature. As I have done throughout this work, I will strive to communicate this material on a nonspecialist's level. I encourage the reader to persevere through those sections that may seem a bit more technical. Nevertheless, the reader should also be advised that each question is self-contained, so a question could be skimmed or skipped altogether without hindering the understanding of other questions or objections.

1. IF THE OPEN VIEW IS CORRECT AND IT IS THE MOST BIBLI-CAL VIEW, WHY HASN'T ANYONE IN CHURCH HISTORY THOUGHT OF IT BEFORE?

First of all, the open view is not altogether new in church history. While little research has yet been done tracing this view throughout history, it seems it was espoused by Calcidius, a fifth-century theologian.[1]

It also appears to have been fairly widespread among nineteenth-century Methodists, as evidenced, for example, by the writings of the chancellor of Ohio Wesleyan University, Lorenzo McCabe, and the popular circuit preacher Billy Hibbard.[2] The view was also espoused, in one form or another, by such noteworthy theologians as G. T. Fechner, Otto Pfeiderer, and Jules Lequier, as well as the great Bible commentator Adam Clarke in the nineteenth century. And, according to some African-American commentators, the open view has been commonly assumed within the African-American Christian tradition.[3]

Still, I must concede that the open view has been relatively rare in church history. In my estimation this is because almost from the start the church's theology was significantly influenced by Plato's notion that God's perfection must mean that he is in every respect unchanging—including in his knowledge and experience. This philosophical assumption has been losing its grip on Western minds over the last hundred years, which is, in part, why an increasing number of Christians are coming to see the significance of the biblical motif on divine openness.

The fundamental issue, however, is the question of how much authority Christians should give to the church tradition. Another way of asking the same question is to ask how much the novelty of a position should count against it in the minds of Christians. The authority of the tradition should, I agree, make all orthodox Christians *cautious* of relatively new positions. We should demand that nontraditional theological perspectives present strong biblical and theological arguments on their behalf before we embrace them. But the authority of tradition should not cause us to automatically rule out a new theological view. This is especially true with regard to the issue of the content of God's

116

foreknowledge. No ecumenical creed of the orthodox church has ever included an article of faith on divine foreknowledge. We are not directly addressing anything central to the traditional definition of orthodoxy, so it seems some flexibility might be warranted.

For example, there has been a long tradition of lively philosophical debate within the church over different views regarding the content and mode of God's omniscience. The church has usually demonstrated a healthy flexibility in allowing for differing perspectives on this matter. For example, St. Jerome questioned (oddly enough) whether God cares enough to know mundane details about the world. No one judged him heretical for doing so. More importantly, there has been a long-standing debate over whether God's omniscience includes knowledge of "counterfactual conditional truths," or what would have happened if certain other things would not have happened. Christian philosophers throughout history have debated whether God's knowledge of contingencies is itself contingent, whether his knowledge is timeless or temporally conditioned, and whether his knowledge of the world is direct or indirect (does God know the world only by knowing himself as its cause, as Augustine and Aquinas taught). So long as omniscience was affirmed, the church has always been open to a variety of new perspectives on this topic. The debate over the openness of the future stands in line with this tradition.

Most importantly for those of us who are Protestant, we must remember that there is no distinctly Protestant belief around today that wasn't at its inception pronounced "new" and often "heretical." For Protestants who confess the Bible as their final authority in matters of faith, the duration of a belief cannot itself settle the question of whether the belief is true. This must be settled by appealing to the authority of Scripture.

Christians from many backgrounds agree that the Lord is restoring his church, preparing his bride for the close of this age and for the ushering in of his eternal kingdom. A central component of this restoration has been God allowing the church to hear and apply his Word in ways that are increasingly free from unbiblical assumptions that previously distorted her hearing and obeying.

For example, Luther recovered the radical nature of divine grace, the centrality of faith, and the priesthood of all believers—crucial aspects of Christianity that had been largely lost since the second and third centuries. Wesley recovered the holy nature of discipleship, which had been dormant for some time. The Pentecostals recovered the relevance of the gifts of the Spirit for today after seventeen hundred years of almost total absence. A number of thinkers throughout this century have been rediscovering the central significance of the doctrine of the Trinity, the understanding that the church is a dynamic organism instead of an organization, and the centrality of eschatology for Christian thought and living.

In each of these instances (and there are others), something "new" was discovered in Scripture—though in truth it wasn't really new at all. It had simply been unnoticed for a long time, sometimes for centuries. Assumptions had crept into the church that had clouded the eyes of believers reading the Word. The result was that aspects of God's self-revelation were obscured. Through the continued prompting of the Spirit, however, God is setting his bride free and giving her a more accurate picture of his identity as well as her own.

I do not intend to put the issue of the openness of God and of the future on par with the reforming movements of Luther, Wesley, or the Pentecostals. I only mean to say that for those who are committed to the Word of God above church tradition, the relative novelty of an opinion can't be conclusive grounds against it. Every view must be judged by its ability to reveal aspects of God's Word to us that we might have previously overlooked. As I attempted to show in chapter 2, I believe that the open view of God does just this.

2. THE BIBLE SOMETIMES USES FIGURES OF SPEECH THAT PORTRAY GOD IN HUMAN TERMS (ANTHROPOMORPHISMS). WHY CAN'T ALL THE VERSES THAT SPEAK OF GOD CHANGING HIS MIND OR EMOTIONS BE UNDERSTOOD ALONG THESE LINES?

Classical theism largely relies on the understanding that all passages describing God as changing are anthropomorphic. Two things may be said in response to this view.

Why Assume Change Is Anthropomorphic?

First, there are certainly passages in the Bible that are figurative and portray God in human terms. You can recognize them because what is said about God is either ridiculous if taken literally (e.g., God has an "outstretched arm," Deut. 4:34; God as "our husband," Hosea 2:2), or because the genre of the passage is poetic (e.g., God has "protecting wings," Ps. 17:8).

However, there is nothing ridiculous or poetic about the way the Bible repeatedly speaks about God changing his mind, regretting decisions, or thinking and speaking about the future in terms of possibilities. These passages usually occur within the historical narrative sections of Scripture. They only strike some as ridiculous because these readers bring to the text a preconception of what God *must* be like. Once one is free from this preconception, these passages contribute to the exalted portrait of the lovingly sovereign God in the Bible. As we saw in chapter 2, such passages occur quite frequently. Though we often fail to see it because of how church tradition has colored the way we read the Bible, the openness of God and of the future constitutes a major motif of Scripture. It is not at all on par with a figure of speech in which God has an outstretched arm or protecting wings.

What Does the Motif of Openness Reveal?

Second, even when the Bible speaks anthropomorphically and figuratively about God, it is speaking truthfully about God. The expressions genuinely tell us true characteristics about God, albeit in a nonliteral fashion. The "arm" of God refers to God's true strength, for example, while his "wings" describe his true protection.

But if we decide that the various accounts of God "changing his mind" are all figurative because we have already decided that God *can't* really do such a thing, what truth do these accounts communicate? If God never changes his mind, saying he does so reveals nothing; it is simply incorrect. If God in truth never anticipates that something is going to happen that turns out not to happen, his telling us that he is sometimes surprised or disappointed (Jer. 3:6–7, 19; Isa. 5:1–7) tells us nothing true; it is simply misleading.

Nor can we explain these verses by claiming that they describe how things *appear* to us but not how they truly are for God, for in many of these passages there is nothing that appears to us. When the inspired Word tells us that God thinks in terms of "perhaps," that God regretted a decision he had made, that God intended to destroy a city but then called it off, or that God expected something to happen that didn't happen, it is telling us things *we would never otherwise know*. The verses cannot be speaking according to appearances, for the subject matter of these texts doesn't appear to us at all.

All the evidence indicates that the verses signifying divine openness should be interpreted every bit as literally as the verses signifying the settledness of the future. Only a preconception of what God can and can't be like would lead us to think otherwise.

3. WHY DO YOU THINK GOD CAN'T FOREKNOW FUTURE FREE ACTIONS?

The most compelling reason for Bible-believing Christians to think this is simply that the Bible depicts God as not knowing future free actions, on the one hand, while also depicting God as knowing all of reality, on the other. This entails that future free decisions do not exist (except as possibilities) for God to know until free agents make them.

If one wants to add philosophical proof on top of this, things get a bit more complicated (to no one's surprise). There are plenty of brilliant philosophers defending the view that God *can,* in principle, foreknow future free actions, and plenty who argue that he cannot, since this constitutes a logical contradiction. I personally am convinced that the best arguments lie in the second camp, but I'm also aware that this isn't an open-and-shut case.

The arguments surrounding this issue are quite technical and discussing them at a philosophical level is outside the parameters of this book. Still, allow me to offer a simplified version of one philosophical argument that attempts to prove that if people are genuinely free, by logical necessity God cannot foreknow as settled their future freely chosen actions.

The Unalterable Future in an Unalterable Past

Everyone agrees that we are not free to change the past. No sane person would claim, for example, that I can now make any free choices about whether John F. Kennedy will be assassinated or not on November 22, 1963. This deed, like all past deeds, has already been accomplished. Indeed, if you were somehow able to take an all-encompassing snapshot of reality on this (or any other) date in the past, thereby capturing on film everything that existed on this date, we would all agree that no one in the present has the power to change any part of it. *Everything* about November 22, 1963, is a "done deal," and no one is now free to alter it.

Now consider, if God has *always* foreknown what I will do in the future, then he certainly knew this on November 22, 1963. His knowledge of my future would thus have been among all the facts of reality captured by our all-encompassing snapshot of reality on this date. But if I am not free to change anything about this snapshot, then I am not free to change anything about God's knowledge of my future contained in this snapshot. This means that I am no more free to change my future than I am free to change anything about November 22, 1963, for the settledness of my future is *part of* the settledness of 1963. I am, in other words, no more free to alter my future than I am free to now prevent John F. Kennedy from being assassinated—if indeed my entire future was settled in God's mind on November 22, 1963.

The Paradox of "God's Book of Known Facts"

It might help to make this a bit more concrete. Suppose for the sake of argument that God decided to reveal to us everything he knew to be true on November 22, 1963. Suppose that on this date God sent down a book from heaven containing all of this information entitled *God's Book of*

Known Facts. Now, if everything you will ever do in the future is listed in this book given on November 22, 1963, and if you are not free in relation to anything in the past, is it not obvious that you could not be free with regard to anything in your future as well? Your whole future is settled in the past—right there in *God's Book of Known Facts.*

To get even more concrete, suppose you read about your future in this book. Let us suppose that among many other things, you read that you will choose to cheat on your taxes on April 12, 2003. This was written on November 22, 1963. Wouldn't you now *feel* the truth that you are no more free to decide your future than you are free to change the past—for you now see your future in the past? How could you possibly believe that it was still up to you to resolve whether or not you would cheat on your taxes on April 12, 2003, when you *know* it is not up to you to resolve any settled fact about November 22, 1963?

Think of it this way. Freedom is the ability to choose between various possibilities. You are free to cheat on your taxes or not only because it is *possible* for you to cheat on your taxes *or not.* But if the fact that you *will* cheat is written in *God's Book of Known Facts,* and God can't possibly be wrong, then it is not possible for you *not* to cheat on your taxes. Hence you cannot be free to choose between the possibilities of cheating or not cheating. In other words, you can't be free.

Ignorance and Reality

Someone might respond to this thought experiment by claiming that God would not reveal such information precisely so that we will remain free. But this response is simply admitting that we only *feel* free because we are *ignorant* of the truth. If we are *truly* free, morally responsible agents, our freedom cannot simply be a feeling based on ignorance.

If we are *truly* free, our ability to determine our future must be rooted in reality. It must *really* be the case that you could choose to cheat or not cheat on your taxes. And this means that what we will freely do cannot be among the facts recorded in *God's Book of Known Facts* on November 22, 1963.

If we are truly free, *God's Book of Known Facts* must be *open to additions* recorded with each free decision we make, just as God "added" fifteen years to Hezekiah's life in response to his prayer (2 Kings 20:6). If we are truly free—if this is in fact part of the way reality really is—there can be nothing beyond possibilities to be recorded until we choose to act on one of those possibilities. We freely *create* the fact and *then* God records it.

If we possess authentic self-determining freedom, then our future must be fundamentally different from our past. The past is unalterable. There are no options for us, which is why we are not free in relation to it. There are no "ifs" or "maybes." Everything about the past is definitely this way and definitely not any other way. If we are free, however, our future must be different from this. It must in part consist of realities that are *possibly* this way or *possibly* that way. Our future must be, at least in part, a realm of possibilities. And the God who knows all of reality just as it is and not otherwise must know it as such. He is not only the God of what will certainly be, he is also the God of possibility.

---

4. IT IS EITHER TRUE OR FALSE THAT I'LL FREELY CHOOSE TO BUY A NEW TAN-COLORED ACURA ON APRIL 17, 2001. IF GOD IS OMNISCIENT, HE MUST KNOW ALL TRUE STATEMENTS AS TRUE AND ALL FALSE STATEMENTS AS FALSE. HENCE, HE

MUST KNOW WHETHER IT'S TRUE OR FALSE THAT I WILL BUY
A TAN-COLORED ACURA IN THE FUTURE ON THIS DATE.

The fact that the Bible frequently depicts God as facing
a partly open future while at the same time consistently affirming his omniscience tells me something is amiss either
with the understanding of omniscience or the understanding of the truth or falsity of future statements presupposed
in this question. I suspect it is the latter.

The most commonly accepted definition of truth is "correspondence with reality." A statement is true if it corresponds with reality, false if it does not. But unless you *assume* that the future already exists, there is nothing for
definitive statements about future free acts to correspond
to. If the future is to some extent open, as we have seen,
then the truth value of a definitive statement about that
open aspect of the future *must itself be open.* That is, it must
be open to being *either* true *or* false until there is in fact a
definite reality that either corresponds to it or not, thus re-
solving it as definitely true or false.

Thus, I deny that the statement "I will choose to buy a
tan-colored Acura on April 17, 2001," is either true or false
(unless, of course, God has indeed predestined this or present causes render it certain). However, if you change your
statement to say that you *may* buy a tan Acura on April 17,
2001, *that* statement is already true or false. Why? Because
there is already a reality that corresponds to it. It is the reality of possibilities.

Possibilities, unlike actualities, are eternal. Whatever has
or ever shall come to pass was always possible, as is whatever could have or might still come to pass. Possibilities are
thus eternally in God's omniscient mind. Hence possibility
statements, and even probability statements about future
free acts, can be true or false in the present and known by
God as such. But definitive statements of open aspects of

the future have nothing to correspond to them and thus are still waiting for their truth value to be resolved.

---

5. Aren't you limiting God by saying he can't know something? Aren't you saying God is ignorant about the future?

Suppose you and I both agree that God is omniscient and thus knows all of reality, but we disagree over, say, the number of trees on a certain plot of land. I say there are 1,300 and you say there are 2,300. You wouldn't say that I am limiting God because he knows fewer trees in my view than he knows in your view. For the issue, of course, isn't about God's knowledge at all; it's about how many trees there are on this plot of land.

This illustrates precisely what is going on regarding the openness debate. The issue is not about God's knowledge at all. Everyone agrees he knows reality perfectly. The issue is the *content* of the reality God perfectly knows—how many things and what kind of things there are on the "plot of land" we call the future.

If everything in the land of the future is settled, then we must all grant that God would perfectly know this. But if there are fewer things in the land of the future that are definite and more things that are possible, then we must grant that God would perfectly know this. It would be illegitimate for the former group to accuse the latter group of limiting God on the grounds that they deny some "definite realities" in the future. So too, it would be illegitimate for the latter group to accuse the former group of limiting God on the grounds that they deny some "possibilities" in the future. The issue is not about the scope or perfection of God's knowledge at all!

Many evangelicals have accused open theists of limiting God by denying that he foreknows the future as exhaustively settled because they assume that the future *is* exhaustively settled. If this assumption is granted, then of course anyone who denied that God foreknew the future as exhaustively settled would be limiting God. But open theists do not share this assumption. The accuracy of the classical assumption that the future is exhaustively settled needs to be examined in the light of Scripture (see chapter 2). Construing this issue as a debate about the perfection of God's knowledge only serves to cloud the issue and instill fear in the minds of people.

6. ISN'T GOD'S WISDOM DIMINISHED BY CLAIMING HE CAN'T FOREKNOW EVERYTHING ABOUT THE FUTURE?

What God "Can't" Do

We wouldn't say that God's greatness is diminished because he "can't" make a round triangle or a married bachelor, for these are self-contradictory concepts. From an open perspective, however, this is what the notion of a "pre-settled" free action is. It is a logical contradiction, and thus it does not insult God's wisdom to say that he "can't" know it.

The Intelligence of Knowing Possibilities

Even beyond this, we should seriously question the assumption that a God who exhaustively foreknows what is definitely going to happen is "wiser" than a God who does not. Reflect for a moment on how unimaginably intelligent a God who faces a partly open future would have to be. Consider the vast number of possibilities you face every day of your life. You could drive one way to work or go a different way. You could wear one outfit or another. You could ask your girlfriend to marry you or not. She could accept your offer or not. You could accept Christ as Lord and Savior or not. The list of possibilities you face each day is voluminous. And with each decision from among all these possibilities, you open up a whole new set of possibilities.

A God who faces a partly open future would know every one of these possibilities from all eternity (for as we said, possibilities, unlike actualities, are eternal). Not only this, but he would also know every possibility that attaches to every possible choice you now have, and every possibility that attaches to each of those possibilities, and so on throughout your life. And he would know this about every possible creature he might create throughout history.

The Infinitely Intelligent Chess Master

We might imagine God as something like an infinitely intelligent chess player. I am told that the average novice chess player can think ahead three or four possible moves. If I do A, for example, my opponent may do B, C, or D. I could then do E, F, or G, to which he may respond with H, I, or J. By contrast, some world-class chess masters can anticipate up to thirty combinations of moves. Now consider that God's perfect knowledge would allow him to anticipate *every* possible move and *every* possible combination of moves, together with *every* possible response he might make to each of them, for *every* possible agent throughout history. And he would be able to do this from eternity past.

Isn't a God who is able to know perfectly these possibilities wiser than a God who simply foreknows or predetermines one story line that the future will follow? And isn't a God who perfectly anticipates and wisely responds to everything a free agent *might* do more intelligent than a God who simply knows what a free agent *will* do? Anticipating and responding to possibilities takes problem-solving intelligence. Simply possessing a crystal ball vision of what's coming requires none.[4]

Which Victory Is Most Praiseworthy?

To return to our chess analogy, consider two chess players. One beats a computerized chessboard because he knows how it was programmed and thus knows every move it *will* make. The other beats a person by anticipating every possible move he *might* make. Which is the more praiseworthy champion? Clearly the latter, for the first victory took very little intelligence. Why, then, should we regard a God who knows all that *will* happen to be wiser than a God who can perfectly anticipate and respond to all that *might* happen?

The Virtue of Novelty and Adventure

The view that God is greater if he possesses exhaustively settled foreknowledge than if he faces a partly open future is questionable on other grounds as well. Consider that in the classical view of foreknowledge, God never experiences novelty, adventure, spontaneity, or creativity. He exists in an eternally static state of unchanging facts. In response to everything that would ever take place in time, he could only say, "Of course, I've known that would happen for an eternity."

Beyond the fact that this perspective is at odds with the basic portrait of God we get in Scripture and radically at odds with the motif of divine openness (see chapter 2), we have to ask: What is admirable about this portrait? Why would this eternally static view of divine knowledge be greater than a view of God enjoying novelty, adventure, spontaneity, creativity, and moment-by-moment personal relationships? If we, who are made in God's image, enjoy these things in some measure, why think that God is great to the extent that his experience is *devoid* of such things? Conversely, if we would experience an eternity utterly devoid of risk and creativity as mundane and perhaps even torturous (I, for one, would), why should we be inclined to think that this is heaven to God?

Can We Enjoy Something God Cannot Enjoy?

One might put my argument this way: If the classical view of divine foreknowledge is correct, there are positive things humans can do that God cannot do. We can enjoy novelty—new songs, fresh poems, original paintings, unanticipated twists in stories, spontaneous play, creative dances, and so on. We can wonder, experience adventure, and enjoy surprises when encountering the unexpected. Though the Bible is explicit in ascribing many of these experiences to God (see chapter 2), the classical view rules them out. Is this not limiting God?

One might respond by saying that we can also sin while God cannot, but this doesn't limit God. The difference between the ability to experience novelty and the ability to experience sin, however, is that the former is positive while the latter is negative. You're not missing out on anything for lacking the latter, but you are if you lack the former. And this is what a limitation is—missing out on something positive.

Another response might be to distinguish between God's knowledge and God's experience. God *knows about* all things ahead of time, one might argue, but his *experience* of them occurs in time. So God enjoys the experience of things he eternally knew were going to happen. There are two problems with this view, however. First, this view still doesn't allow God to experience novelty and risk. The experience of these things depends on not knowing with certainty what is going to come to pass. Second, this view is actually incompatible with the classical view of foreknowledge. Experience is the richest form of knowledge. If God's experience of an event adds *anything* to God's foreknowledge of it, then his foreknowledge of that event was not complete. The classical view of foreknowledge rules this out, for it holds that God's knowledge of the future cannot be improved in any respect. Indeed, if one holds the classical view of divine foreknowledge consistently, it is difficult to see how God could even distinguish his foreknowledge of the event from the actual occurrence of it. *Any* change between God's foreknowing and God's experience implies that *something* was added to God's knowledge.

The Legacy of Plato

The problem, as I see it, is that since Plato, Western philosophy has been infatuated with the idea of an unchanging, timeless reality. Time and all change were considered less real and less good than the unchanging timeless realm. Time is simply the "moving shadow" of eternity, according to Plato.[5] This infatuation with the "unchanging" unfortunately crept into the church early on and has colored the way Christians look at the world, read their Bibles, and develop their theology.[6] We have thus been subtly conditioned to assume that possibilities, openness, change, and contingency are "beneath" God. As with Plato, we tend to assume that they are only aspects of the "lower" reality where imperfect humans live. *We* experience the future as somewhat open only because we are limited beings.

I submit to you that sound biblical interpretation as well as sound philosophical reflection suggests that this Platonic assumption is misguided. Simple observation shows us that the higher up a being is in the scale of things, the *more* possibilities are open to it, the *more* spontaneity it evidences, and the *more* sensitive it is to change. People, for example, generally have more possibilities open to them than cats, evidence more freedom in their lives than dogs, and can sense another person's mood and respond accordingly better than gorillas.

If God is indeed the *greatest* conceivable being, why should we not conclude that God would have *more* possibilities open to him, would be *more* free, and would be *more* sensitive to change than we humans? The Platonic and classical Christian notion that God (and therefore God's knowledge) must be utterly unchanging contradicts this. Everything we read in Scripture and everything we observe in the world around us suggests that a God who is frozen in an eternity of perfectly certain facts is inferior to the God of the possible, who is capable of discovery, risk, novelty, and adventure.

7. YOUR THEOLOGY SEEMS TO LIMIT GOD TO TIME. BUT GOD CREATED TIME WHEN HE CREATED THE UNIVERSE. DOESN'T THIS ENTAIL THAT HE IS ABOVE TIME?

God and Sequence

Of course God is "above time," for our concept of time is simply the way we measure change. This doesn't mean, however, that there is no *sequence* in God's experience. A fundamental aspect of classical theological thinking, again revealing the influence of Plato, was that God experiences no "before" or "after." He experiences all of time in a single, changeless, eternal moment. We have to ask, however, Where is this notion taught in the Bible? Doesn't every page of the Bible paint a portrait of a God who experiences things, thinks things, and responds to things *sequentially?* Every verb applied to God in the Bible testifies to this. The God of the Bible is alive, dynamic, personal, changing, free, and relational. How different this is from the static, unchanging, wholly necessary God of Plato and much of the church's classical theology.

The Personal God of Scripture

The view that there is no sequence to God's experience not only contradicts our reading of Scripture, it also undermines our confidence in God's responsiveness to prayer. Indeed, I believe it subtly erodes our conviction that God's personal, moment-by-moment involvement in our lives is real. Try to get a coherent conception of a personal God who is nonsequential; it can't be done. Plato was more consistent in construing this "being" as an impersonal principle and Aristotle more consistent in calling him "the unmoved mover." The church's primary theologians (e.g., Augustine and Aquinas) were inconsistent in trying to fuse this impersonal philosophical concept with the dynamic God of history who responsively interacts with people on a moment-by-moment basis.

---

8. DOESN'T EINSTEIN'S THEORY OF RELATIVITY PROVE THAT TIME IS ULTIMATELY UNREAL, THUS DISPROVING THE IDEA THAT GOD EXPERIENCES A PAST OR FUTURE?

The theory of relativity dictates that the measurement (or experience) of time depends on the relative traveling speeds of two observers as well as their distance from one another. The passage of time for one cannot be exactly correlated with the passage of time for the other. Since we are all finite observers, we cannot speak meaningfully about a single time that encompasses everything. This much Einstein's theory proves. But his theory does not address how an *omnipresent* observer like God would or would not experience time. Einstein was a scientist, not a theologian, and his theory is about empirical, not divine, reality.

Stated differently, Einstein's theory is concerned only with the transference of information at the speed of light between finite observers. But God is not one finite observer among others. He is an observer who is contemporaneous with every finite observer. This changes everything (though we shouldn't fault Einstein for not incorporating this into his theory).

It means that God's experience of others is not dependent on (relative to) the speed of light. He doesn't need to "wait" for information to arrive to him via the speed of light. He is "there" when the information originates. This means that for God—but for no one else—there *can* be an all-embracing "now" in which all the relative "nows" experienced by finite observers coincide. While each finite observer experiences the "now" of another finite observer relative to their distance from that observer and their own speed of travel relative to the speed of light, God experiences the "now" that is contemporaneous with *every* observer.

Einstein showed that for finite observers there can be no meaningful talk of an all-encompassing time, for *within the physical cosmos* we have no frame of reference to make sense of such talk. For those of us who believe in an omnipresent God, however, there *is* a meaningful frame of reference for such talk. We can't step out of our finitude, but we are related to a God who transcends our finitude.

9. Why would God create a world with free wills he can't meticulously control or foreknow, a world

THAT ALLOWS PEOPLE TO OPPOSE HIS WILL, HURT OTHER
PEOPLE, AND DAMN THEMSELVES?

This question assumes that it would have been better to create a world in which there were no free wills, in which people could never oppose God's will, hurt other people, or damn themselves. Such a world would on one level be "perfect," but it would also be perfectly robotic. God would get everything he wants, except the one thing he *really* wants—namely, agents who freely *choose* to participate in his triune love. Love has to be chosen, and this means that love is inherently risky. Reason, intuition, and certainly experience tell us this is true.

Consider this example: Suppose you possessed the technological knowledge to program a computer chip and secretly implant it in your spouse's brain while he or she was sleeping. This chip would cause your spouse to talk and act exactly as you would want, though your spouse would still think he or she was choosing to talk and act this way. That person would, on one level, be "the perfect spouse." The loving behavior and words would be exactly what you desire. You would, in fact, know exactly what your spouse was going to say and do before he or she did. After all, you programmed the responses.

We might enjoy such an arrangement for a while, but wouldn't you eventually grow tired of it? Wouldn't it be unfulfilling? For you would know that everything your spouse was saying and doing to you, as wonderful as it might be, was really *you saying and doing to yourself.* Your spouse may *speak* and *act* loving toward you, but he or she would not *truly be* loving you. It would all be a charade. There would, in fact, be no real person, no thinking, feeling, and willing agent, who would be intentionally *choosing* to love you on his or her own. The fact that your spouse would experience himself or herself as choosing to love doesn't change this, for this experience also is simply due to the sophistication of your programming. Your spouse's sense of free will is an illusion. For love to be real, it must really be possible to choose against it.

This illustration demonstrates that love *must* be chosen. It could not be otherwise. It's part of its very definition. As a triangle must have three sides and all bachelors must be unmarried, so love must be chosen. This means that love is, by its very nature, risky. To create a cosmos populated with free agents (angels and humans) who are capable of choosing love requires that God create a cosmos in which beings can choose to oppose his will, hurt other people, and damn themselves. If love is the goal, this is the price.

The solution to the problem of evil, I believe, is found in this insight.

---

10. EVEN IF ALL EVIL COMES FROM FREE WILLS, AND EVEN IF GOD CAN'T FOREKNOW WHAT THESE WILLS ARE GOING TO CHOOSE, ISN'T GOD STILL RESPONSIBLE FOR THEIR CHOICES SINCE HE CREATED THEM? ISN'T ALL THE EVIL OF THE WORLD STILL HIS FAULT?

In a general sense, the Creator must be responsible for everything that transpires in his creation. He unilaterally decided that the risk of free agents choosing evil, breaking his heart, and bringing nightmarish suffering upon themselves and others was worth it. He is responsible for creating a cosmos that was capable of this. This doesn't imply that it is his fault if and when these agents freely choose evil courses of action, however. If agents are truly self-determining, God is not responsible for the individual evil choices that these agents make.

In a small way, we do the exact same thing when we have children. We know (or at least should know) all the risks involved—we and others may get hurt. Love is risky, but we decide to accept the risk and bring children into the world because we judge that love is worth the risk. In this sense, we are responsible for their lives. But the more our children become autonomous, self-determining, morally responsible agents, the less responsibility parents have for the choices their children make. To the extent that they act out of their self-determining freedom, what they choose is not to our credit (when it is good) or our blame (when it is evil).

If people truly believed that the risk of pain wasn't worth it, they would never have children and never enter into loving relationships. Indeed, if they were totally consistent, they would terminate their lives. Every day we choose not to commit suicide we are manifesting our fundamental conviction that life *is* worth it, despite all the pain we may experience. And if *we* decide daily that the risk of life and love is worth the risk of pain, how can we question God's decision to create such a world?

11. IF LOVE HAS TO BE CHOSEN, AS YOU HOLD, DID GOD HAVE TO CHOOSE TO BE LOVING?

The Bible tells us that God cannot lie, carry out any evil, or be other than he is regarding his perfect character (Num. 23:19; Heb. 6:18; James 1:13, 17). As for his defining attributes of greatness, God is eternally the same. (But note, the Bible doesn't say that God's *experiences* are eternally the same; it suggests just the opposite.) The Bible also shows us that humans (and angels) are not like this. We can, by God's grace, become holy, or we can resist God's work in our lives and remain sinful. We can, by our choices, build a loving or an unloving character. Unlike God, what we ultimately become is not built into what we are as a matter of necessity. Rather, we are beings who have to *decide* what we will become. This is what it means to be *self*-determining.

Sound philosophizing leads us to the same conclusion. Aristotle wisely taught that what is eternal cannot be other than it is. It is (as philosophers say) "necessary." To be able to become other than you presently are means your nature is not eternal. You are (as philosophers again say) "contingent." This constitutes one major difference between God and all created beings. Regarding his character, God is who he is from all eternity (he is "necessary"), while the free agents he creates must *choose* their eternal natures (we are "contingent"). This is why we, but not God, must go through this probational stage of existence we now find ourselves in. To participate in God's eternal triune love that he has by nature, we must choose it.

12. THE EMPHASIS THAT THE OPEN VIEW PLACES ON FREE WILL UNDERMINES GOD'S GRACE. IF OUR WILL DETERMINES WHETHER OR NOT WE ARE SAVED, THEN SALVATION IS TO SOME EXTENT A "WORK." BUT SCRIPTURE SAYS WE ARE SAVED TOTALLY BY GOD'S GRACE—EVEN OUR FAITH IS A GIFT FROM GOD (EPH. 2:8).

I will offer three points to suggest that there is no inconsistency in maintaining that salvation is completely due to God's grace, on the one hand, while affirming that free will has a role to play in salvation, on the other.

First, consider the implication of denying that human choice plays any role in salvation. If the reason why some people are saved and other people are not isn't because some people choose to accept God's grace while others refuse it, then the reason must be because God chooses some people to be saved and others not to be. But this contradicts Scripture's teaching that God's love is universal and impartial and that he wants everyone to be saved (Ezek. 18:23, 32; 33:11; Acts 10:34; 1 Tim. 2:4; 4:10; 2 Peter 3:9; 1 John 2:2). If God genuinely desires all to be saved, the reason why some are not must be because they don't accept salvation, while those who are saved do accept it.

Second, there is no reason to think that accepting a gift is "work." If someone offers me a hundred dollars and I accept it, I did not thereby work to earn the gift! So too, the fact that humans must accept God's gracious gift of salvation does not mean that we "work" for it. Scripture is clear that we cannot work to earn God's grace—that is a contradiction in terms (see Rom. 4:4–16). But it is also clear from Scripture that we do need to accept it: "I have set before you life and death, blessings and curses," the Lord says. And then he admonishes us to "choose life" (Deut. 30:19).

How can we even choose to accept salvation, however, if we are "dead" in sin (Eph. 2:1)? And if we choose to believe or not, how can Scripture say that faith is a gift of God (Eph. 2:8; see also John 6:44–65; 1 Cor. 12:4)? This leads to my third point. There is no question that fallen humans would never choose to accept God's offer of salvation were it not for the work of the Holy Spirit in our lives. We are, on our own, so in bondage to sin and the devil that our "natural" orientation is rebellion against God. We are "slaves" to sin and the devil (Rom. 6:6, 16–17; Gal. 4:8). It is one thing to say that the gracious work of the Holy Spirit is *necessary* for our salvation, however, and another to say that it is *sufficient* for our salvation. The Holy Spirit makes it *possible* for us to believe, but he does not make it *impossible not* to believe. Scripture makes it clear that people can—and do—resist the work of the Holy Spirit in their lives (e.g., Isa. 63:10; Luke 7:30; Acts 7:51; Eph. 4:30; Heb. 3:8, 15; 4:7).

From all of this it follows that if a person is saved, they have only God to thank for it, while if they are not, they have only themselves to blame.

13. In Romans 9, Paul teaches that God "has mercy on whomever he chooses, and he hardens whomever he chooses" (v. 18). This choice does not depend "on human will or exertion," but simply on God's sovereign will (v. 16). He is the potter and we are his clay (vv. 21–22), and the vessels made of clay have no right to ask God, "Why have you made me like this?" (v. 20). The understanding that election is based on God's sovereign will, not on human will, contradicts the open view.

At first glance, it may seem that these passages from Romans 9 contradict the open view of God. Clearly, if salvation and damnation are ultimately due to God's will, it cannot be the case that the future salvation or damnation of people is undecided until they freely choose to accept or reject God's gracious offer of salvation. I will refer to this interpretation of Romans 9 as the "deterministic interpretation," for in this view God alone determines who will receive mercy. I will offer six considerations that argue against this interpretation. My first two points are preliminary reflections that set Romans 9 in a broader context. The last four are deeper reflections on the meaning of this passage.

First, it should be noted that the deterministic interpretation of Romans 9 contradicts not only the open view of God and the future but classical Arminianism as well. Everyone who believes that God desires all to be saved and that free will has any role in determining whether a person is saved or not must come to terms with this passage.

Second, the view that God simply determines who will and will not receive mercy contradicts the teaching of Scripture that God's love is universal and impartial and that he desires everyone to be saved (Acts 10:34; 1 Tim. 2:4; 2 Peter 3:9).[7] This implies that we are misinterpreting this passage if we think it teaches that God's will is decisive in determining who will be saved and who will be damned.

Third, whenever we attempt to understand a complex line of reasoning such as we find in Romans 9, it is important to pay close attention to the author's own summary of his argument, if and when he provides one. Fortunately, Paul provides us with such a summary. Unfortunately for the deterministic interpretation, however, it appeals to free will as the decisive factor in determining who "receives mercy" and who gets "hardened." Paul begins his summary by asking, "What then are we to say?" (v. 30). If the deterministic interpretation were correct, we would expect Paul to answer this question with a statement such as this: "The sovereign God determines who will be elect and who will not, and no one has the right to question him." This is not the case, however. He summarizes his argument in this chapter by concluding:

> Gentiles, who did not strive for righteousness, have attained it, that is, righteousness through faith; but Israel, who did strive for the righteousness that is based on the law, did not succeed in fulfilling that law. Why not? Because they did not strive for it on the basis of faith, but as if it were based on works (vv. 30–32).

Paul explains everything he's been talking about in this chapter by appealing to the morally responsible choices of the Israelites and Gentiles. The Jews did not "strive" by faith, though they should have (see Rom. 10:3). Instead, they chose to trust in their own works. This theme recurs throughout chapters 9 through 11. As a nation, Paul says, the Jews "were broken off *because of their unbelief*" (11:20). *This* is why they have now been hardened (Rom. 11:7, 25), while the Gentiles who seek God by faith have been "grafted in" (11:23).

We see that God's process of hardening some and having mercy on others is not arbitrary: God expresses "severity toward those who have fallen [the nation of Israel], but kindness toward you [believers], provided you continue in his kindness" (11:22).

Fourth, if read in the light of its Old Testament background, Paul's analogy of a potter working with clay doesn't imply that the potter unilaterally decides everything, as the deterministic interpretation of Romans 9 suggests. Indeed, in the passage that makes the most extensive use of this analogy, Jeremiah 18, it has the *opposite* connotation. As we saw in chapter 2, the point of the analogy in Jeremiah is that the Lord is able and willing to adjust his plans with people just as a potter revises his plans for a "vessel" once his original plan "was spoiled" (Jer. 18:4–6). Because he is the potter and has the right to fashion clay as he sees fit, he will "change his mind" about his intentions to bless or curse a nation if that nation changes its ways, for better or for worse (18:7–11).

The point of the analogy for both Jeremiah and Paul is not that the "clay" God works with is passive in the hands of the potter, but rather that the wise potter has the authority and power to revise his plans regarding what he wants to fashion depending on what the clay does. If people turn from following him, God revises his plan to fashion them as vessels of mercy. If people repent of their sin, God revises his plans to fashion them as vessels of judgment. The Jews who trusted in their works and rejected Christ are examples of the former. The Gentiles who turned to Christ are examples of the latter.

So when Paul says that God "has mercy on whomever he chooses, and he hardens the heart of whomever he chooses" (Rom. 9:18), he is not suggesting that God does this without any consideration of the choices people make. The people God chooses to have mercy on are those who have faith. The people God chooses to harden are those who don't "strive for [righteousness] on the basis of faith, but as if it were based on works" (v. 32).

This explains why Paul says that God "endured with much patience" the vessels he was preparing for destruction (v. 22). Why would he need "much patience" if the vessel was "spoiled" by his own fashioning? Why would he say, "All day long I have held out my hands to a disobedient and contrary people" (10:21; citing Isa. 65:2) if he was the one molding them to be disobedient in the first place?

This leads to our fifth point. When Paul responds to the charge of injustice by asking, "who . . . are you, a human being, to argue with God?" (v. 20), he is not thereby appealing to the sheer power of the potter over the clay. He is rather appealing to the rights and wisdom of the potter to fashion clay according to his providential purposes ("as seem[s] good to him" [Jer. 18:4]), and in a manner that is appropriate, given the kind of clay he has to work with.

This fashioning may *look* arbitrary to Jews who believed that they were the "vessel of honor" simply by virtue of being Jewish or because of their works, but it is not. It is based on whether or not one is willing to seek after the righteousness of God that comes by faith, not works (9:30–32; 10:3–5, 12–13; 11:22–23).

Sixth, and perhaps most importantly, it is crucial that we interpret Romans 9 according to the question Paul is attempting to answer. Paul's interest in this chapter is not to show that God chooses who will and will not be saved. The issue Paul wrestles with throughout chapters 9, 10, and 11 is whether or not "the word of God [his covenantal promises] failed"(9:6).

As we have already suggested, to Jews of Paul's time who assumed that God's covenant with them was based on their works, the Christian message of salvation by faith in Christ implied that God had broken his covenantal promises to them. It seemed that "the word of God failed." Paul refutes this by pointing out that God's covenantal promises have never been based on works. This is why "not all Israelites truly belong to Israel" and "not all of Abraham's children are his true descendants" (9:6–7). You can be a Jew and not belong to God's covenant, for it is faith and not works that make one a true Israelite. For the same reason, one can be a Gentile and yet belong to God's covenant (see Rom. 2:28–29).

To those who always assumed that their works were the basis of God's promise, this seems unjust, but Paul insists that God has the right to choose *whomever he wants,* just as he did when he chose Jacob over Esau without any consideration for their works (Rom. 9:10–13). No one has the right to second-guess him (vv. 14, 19–20). He is the potter and we are the clay. If he chooses to have mercy on sinners simply because they have faith, that is his divine prerogative. If he chooses to harden people "because of their unbelief" (11:20), that too is his prerogative. God's criterion of justice does not have to answer to our criterion of justice.

I conclude, then, that the deterministic interpretation of Romans 9 is incorrect. When read in context, Romans 9 is not incompatible with affirming human free will, and thus not incompatible with the open view of God and the future. Open theists as well as classical Arminians can unequivocally affirm that God "has mercy on whomever he chooses, and he hardens the heart of whomever he chooses" (9:18). Following Paul, we simply conclude that the "whomever" in this verse refers to "all who choose to believe" and "all who do not."

14. HOW CAN YOU CLAIM THAT THE FUTURE IS *PARTLY* OPEN AND *PARTLY* SETTLED? IT SEEMS LIKE YOU'RE TRYING TO HAVE YOUR CAKE AND EAT IT TOO.

As mentioned in chapter 1, the claim that the future is partly open and partly settled initially strikes many people as contradictory. As a matter of fact, however, there is nothing contradictory about it. Indeed, as we argued in chapter 1, we assume that the future is partly open and partly settled with every decision we make. I can't genuinely deliberate between options unless I assume that (a) most of the future that surrounds the issue I'm deliberating over is predictable and not up to me to decide; and (b) the matter I am deliberating *is* genuinely "open" and "up to me" to resolve. In short, we all *live* as if the future was partly open and partly settled.

The main explanation for why so many assume that the future must be totally one way or the other—despite our universal experience to the contrary—is because of the vast influence of Plato in Western culture. When we assume that the future is exhaustively settled, we mistakenly assume that anyone who denies this must hold the opposite extreme—that the future is exhaustively unsettled. Scripture, reason, and experience suggest, however, that the truth lies in the middle of these extremes.

Another possible explanation for why some Christians assume that the future must be exhaustively settled is that they cannot conceive of how God could control the world as effectively as he does unless he knew all the future as settled. I grant that it takes an incomprehensibly wise God to be sovereign over a world populated with a myriad of free agents, each having a degree of say-so in what transpires. I can thus appreciate the natural inclination to bring God down to our limited comprehension and assume that he must meticulously control or at least foreknow all that is going to take place in order to protect his sovereignty. But out of fidelity to Scripture (see chapter 2) and reverence for the incomprehensible sovereignty of God, I submit that this is a temptation we must resist. Above all, we must let God be God.

15. IN YOUR VIEW, HOW MUCH OF THE FUTURE IS OPEN AND HOW MUCH IS SETTLED? AND HOW DOES A PERSON KNOW WHAT IS OPEN AND WHAT IS NOT, ESPECIALLY AS IT CONCERNS HIS OR HER OWN LIFE?

Scripture shows that the future is settled concerning God's acquisition of a bride (the church) who will participate in his triune love throughout eternity. Scripture also shows that the future is settled regarding God's ultimate victory over Satan and all forces of evil who have aligned themselves with him. Scripture also shows that God providentially determines particular future events to the extent required for his ultimate goals to be attained.

At the same time, Scripture shows that the future is open to the extent that God has granted humans and angels free will. More particularly, Scripture shows that whatever occurs against God's will was at some point in the past open, for it should not have happened and did not need to happen.

Beyond Scripture's specific accounts, however, things become much more ambiguous. A good deal can be predicted about the future simply on the basis of the laws of nature (including human nature), consequences of past decisions, genetic and environmental forces that influence human life, and the like. Conversely, some openness in the future can be discerned by the way we deliberate about future decisions and can be seen in recent scientific findings (e.g., quantum theory). But regarding *the specifics* of any individual's life at any given point in time, I see no way to know for certain what is and is not open.

This should not be surprising. Consider how difficult it is for legal courts to isolate the morally responsible freedom of a defendant from genetic and environmental factors that conditioned his or her freedom. It's exceedingly difficult for us to discern this even about ourselves, for all these factors are interwoven so tightly that they form a single "whole" self.

If we factor into the equation the character we have been acquiring by our choices, the matter becomes more complex still. If we also factor in the constant influence of God's invisible providential hand and the influence of good and evil spiritual forces on our lives, we begin to get some idea of just how complex and unknowable the extent of our freedom really is. When all is said and done, only God can know the extent to which individuals at any given moment act out of their self-determining free will as opposed to extraneous influences in their lives.

Having said this, allow me to offer a word of practical advice. The fact that Scripture commands us to take authority over our thoughts and behavior tells us that through the empowering of the Holy Spirit, we are capable of rising above the determined circumstances in our lives to make choices in conformity with God's will. We will make no progress in spiritual development if we buy into the prevalent "victim mentality" of our current culture and try to blame factors and forces outside ourselves for the way we are. Genes, environment, parenting, and spiritual forces do *condition* who we are. But for believers whose spirits have been regenerated by the Spirit of God, these conditioning factors cannot *determine* who we are unless *we choose* to allow them to do so.

The operating assumption for the believer, then, must be that the future is open *insofar as we can choose it*. Most importantly, we must choose to rely on and cooperate with God to bring about the possibilities for our future that he sees as being best for us and best for the kingdom of love he is building through us. Empowered and led by the God of the possible, we must courageously step out of the bondages that constrain us and step into the possibilities he opens up for us.

16. The open view seems to put God at the mercy of free decisions and demeans his sovereignty.

The Sovereign God Who Gives Power to Others

It is true that in the open view, as in classical Arminianism, much of what transpires in world history is the result of the decisions of free agents, not God's will. This is why world history with all of its horrors does not clearly reflect God's beautiful character. Humans and fallen angels can—and do—thwart God's will for their own lives and interfere with God's will for others.

But just because God does not always get his way does not mean that God is "at the mercy" of free decisions or that his sovereignty is demeaned. In contrast to those who hold to process theology, open theists and classical Arminians believe that God chose to create this world and give agents power to resist him if they so choose. In making this decision, God temporarily limited his own ability to unilaterally get his way. As Scripture clearly shows, however, God has not given away more power to creatures than he can handle. That would obviously be an unwise decision and thus one that is impossible for an all-wise God to make. It is therefore inaccurate to say that the Creator is at the "mercy" of anything or anyone—even though he has set things up so that his will can be frustrated and his heart broken by what his free creatures do.

Sovereignty and Control

Does this view demean God's sovereignty? On the contrary, *it establishes it*. Many Christians use the word "sovereignty" as though it were synonomous with "control." Hence, any view that does not portray God as controlling everything is "denying the sovereignty of God." The fact that this charge is so frequently raised against the open view (and against classical Arminianism as well) is evidence of the pervasiveness of the unfortunate equation of "sovereignty" with "control."

But why should we consider "control" the most exalted view of divine sovereignty? Can we not conceive of a more praiseworthy way that God might choose to rule (be sovereign over) the creation? If we take our model of divine sovereignty from the Bible instead of from the natural inclination of fallen humans to exalt power and control, what we discover is that God's sovereignty is a sovereignty of love. God demonstrates divine power when he empowers others to make choices to either enter into a loving relationship with him or not. He demonstrates divine power when he thereby puts himself in a position in which his heart might grieve because of the adultery of his beloved (Hosea 11). Most importantly, he demonstrated divine power when Christ came to earth and allowed himself to be crucified for sinners. *This* is what it is for God to have power and authority, and *this* ought to be the model by which we exercise power within the body of Christ (Luke 22:24–27; Eph. 5:25–27; Phil. 2: 5–8).

Controlling Because You Can

It takes a truly self-confident, sovereign God to make himself vulnerable. It takes a God who is truly in authority to give away some of his control, knowing that doing so might cause him incredible pain. By contrast, to simply control others so that you always get your way is the surest sign of insecurity and weakness. To do so simply because you *can* demonstrates nothing praiseworthy about one's character—unless you're inclined to worship sheer power and control.

I have total unilateral control over how my toes wiggle, for example. But would anyone consider me praiseworthy, or even slightly virtuous, because of this? Obviously not. For it takes no character to exercise an innate power. Of course I can wiggle my toes; they are mine! But why, then, would we think it glorious that God "wiggles" his creation as he pleases, even "wiggling" millions to eternal suffering (in the theology of Calvinism), *just because he can?* Of course God could "wiggle" his creation however he chooses if this is what he wanted to do; it is, after all, his creation. But what is glorious about this?

How different, and how much more glorious, is the portrait of a God who chooses to create a cosmos populated with free agents. Out of love, God empowers others to be personal beings. Out of love, he respects their God-given ability to make decisions even when doing so causes him pain. Out of love for his whole creation, he wisely weaves their free decisions into his general providential plan. Finally, out of love he becomes one of them and dies for them that they might eternally share in his love. *That* is divine sovereignty!

Despite the various claims made by some today that we must protect "the sovereignty of God" by emphasizing his absolute control over creation and thus by denouncing the open view, I submit that we ought to denounce the view that God exercises total control over everything for this very same reason: *It demeans the sovereignty of God.*

17. How can you trust a God who is uncertain about the future?

God's Confidence about the Future

First of all, it is not accurate to say the open view entails that God is "uncertain about the future." God knows all future possibilities throughout eternity. He is certain about everything that could be and thus is never caught off guard. God is also perfectly certain about a good deal of what is actually going to take place in the future, for he knows what he is planning on doing and he knows perfectly all the necessary consequences of present decisions. He is certain enough about what *will* and what *may* occur that he can assure us that his overall plans for creation will be attained.

Recall that in the open view, God is the author of the "Choose Your Own Adventure" story of world history (see chapter 1). He predetermines and thus foreknows the general structure of the story as a whole as well as how each individual story may go, depending on what a given individual chooses. He predetermines and thus foreknows whatever details he needs to in order to ensure that the overall plot stays on course. For all these reasons, it is not accurate to say that God "is uncertain about the future" in the open view. There is a degree of openness in the future, but God is absolutely certain about the range of possibilities contained in this openness, for he is the one who created it.

Trusting a God Who Can Alter the Future

Some might insist that you can trust a God who knows every detail about what will occur in the future more than one for whom significant parts of it are known only as possibilities. This claim is frequently made, but it strikes me as altogether unfounded. Indeed, I would argue that the classical view, if thought through consistently, actually offers believers *less* security than the open view.

Let us suppose God foreknows that in two days you are going to be beaten and robbed while walking in the park. In the classical view of foreknowledge, if God really foreknows this, there's nothing you can do about it. It is certain, for God's knowledge is certain. Indeed, in the classical view there has never been a moment in all eternity when it wasn't certain that this exact event would happen to you on this exact date. How does believing this help you "trust God"? What are you really trusting God for? To simply know from all eternity that this terrible event is going to happen to you? What security is there in that? How does this belief help you in the least?

Most people do not follow their belief that God possesses exhaustively settled foreknowledge to its logical conclusion, however. Instead, they believe that you can trust a God who foreknows everything more than a God who doesn't because a God who foreknew that this terrible event was going to happen to you could warn you about it or otherwise prevent it from happening. Think about this, however. Do you see a problem here? If God warned you not to go walking in that park two days from now, he obviously *didn't* foreknow from all eternity that you were going to get robbed and beaten in the park. If God foreknew it from all eternity, it couldn't be altered. What people who talk this way really believe is that God foreknew that you *might* get robbed, depending on what you did. He knew that you would get robbed and beaten *if* you went to that park, but also that you wouldn't get robbed and beaten *if* you listened to his prompting and stayed home. Clearly, God foreknew *possibilities* in this account, not *certainties*. And *this* is the real reason why people feel they can trust a God who has foreknowledge.

Notice, this is precisely what the open view asserts and the classical view denies about God. In the open view, God knows all possibilities and all probabilities (as well as all settled realities) perfectly. Because God's foreknowledge consists in part of possibilities, not certainties, he can be trusted to inspire us to avoid certain future possibilities he sees coming.[8] In the open view account of this episode, therefore, God could have seen that it was becoming more and more likely that you were going to take a stroll in the park where this robber was likely to be hanging out. He knows the thoughts and intentions of all individuals perfectly and can play them out in his mind like an infinitely wise chess master anticipating every possible combination of moves his opponent could ever make. It would thus be no problem for him to see the likelihood, if not (at this point) the certainty, that this ordeal would happen unless he intervened.

Now let us assume you are a person who frequently talks and listens to God. What is more, you have family and friends who pray for you on a consistent basis. For the God who has designed the world so that prayer makes a great difference in how things transpire (see chapter 3), this is no minor consideration. Prayer opens the door for God to sovereignly alter what otherwise would come to pass. And the happy result is that a robbery that might have occurred was prevented.

That, I submit, is a God you can trust. Trusting God to make a difference in our future only makes sense if the future is for us *and for him* partly open. Only if God is the God of what *might be* and not only the God of what *will be* can we trust him to steer us away from what *should not be* and in the direction of what *should be*.

---

18. IF GOD ISN'T IN CONTROL OF EVERYTHING, THE WORLD FEELS UNSAFE. IF THE FUTURE IS OPEN AND IF THINGS CAN HAPPEN OUTSIDE OF GOD'S WILL, WHAT GUARANTEE IS THERE THAT THERE IS A POINT TO A PERSON'S SUFFERING? MAYBE IT'S ALL JUST BAD LUCK.

My experience has been that many of those who honestly examine the evidence for the open view and choose to reject it do so not because the evidence is weak but because they fear its implications. It is true that according to the open view things can happen in our lives that God didn't plan or even foreknow with certainty (though he always foreknew they were possible). This means that in the open view things can happen to us that have no overarching divine purpose. In this view, "trusting in God" provides no assurance that everything that happens to us will reflect his divine purposes, for there are other agents who also have power to affect us, just as we have power to affect others. This, it must be admitted, can for some be a scary thought. I am sympathetic to the reaction, but I also believe there are several considerations that can effectively address it from an open perspective.

Fear and Truth

First, how is the scariness of a view relevant to the question of whether or not the view is true? There is no reason to conclude that something is true to the extent that it conforms to our wishes. Indeed, the fact that the open view *doesn't* conform to what we might wish were true actually provides one more reason for thinking that it *is* true, for reality rarely conforms to our wishes. If we are honest, our core belief about the world—manifested not by what we *say* but by what we *do*—is that it *is* sometimes a scary place.

Whatever view of God we might embrace, we still lock our doors at night. We take steps to protect ourselves and our loved ones from harm. This is wise, for a world in which innocent kids of godly parents can get kidnapped or killed by drunk drivers is scary. We all already know this. The open view simply articulates what we already believe at a core level. Just look at how we *act*.

Divine Control and Comfort

Second, I do not see how affirming an all-controlling God provides any real comfort in the face of the scary aspects of the world. Suppose there has been a string of robberies and beatings in your neighborhood. You are understandably concerned about your safety and the safety of your children. How does believing that every robbery and beating was ordained by God help you cope with this fear? You're still going to go out and buy an extra padlock for your door and bars for your windows. You still know this evil *could* happen to you, unless you take precautions. You still know at the core of your being that the world is just as scary with your belief as without it. So to what advantage is your belief?

Indeed, I would submit that your belief actually makes the world a scarier place. For one thing, if God controls robbers and these robbers victimize godly and ungodly people alike (which no one can deny), then it might be that God has decided to have one of these robbers victimize your family. If God has decided this, there is nothing you can do about it. If God is the sort of God who is capable of ordaining such evils, then you can't trust God's character. You have nothing to hang on to. If God ordained that one house be robbed, he could just as easily ordain that your house is next. If God ordained that one child be kidnapped, he could just as easily ordain that your child will be next. If God controls all things, there's *nothing* you can do about it if he has, in fact, decided this.

If God chooses not to control all things, however, then there *is* something you can do about it. As a morally responsible free person, you can make choices that maximize your safety and minimize your vulnerability against other free people who have chosen evil. The world is perhaps still scary, but less so than if the Creator himself had the kind of character that made him willing to ordain child kidnappings and the power to ensure that what he ordains will certainly be accomplished.

Find Comfort in the Trials

Finally, and most importantly, in the face of a scary world, the open view offers the same comfort that the New Testament offers. With Scripture, the open view affirms that God's character is unambiguously loving and thus that he is on your side. He doesn't ordain evil. This view affirms that, regardless of what happens to you, your eternal relationship with the Lord is secure (Rom. 8:31–39).

Furthermore, the open view affirms that Christ will be with us to provide a peace that "surpasses all understanding" whatever may come our way (Phil. 4:7). It affirms that whatever happens, God will work with us to bring a redemptive purpose out of the event (Rom. 8:28). The open view also affirms that God can alter your destiny, precisely because the open view holds that the future is in part *not* settled. Finally, the open view affirms with Scripture the central hope that when God's kingdom is established, it will have been worth it.

The world is still scary. It is in a state of war, under siege by the enemy of our souls, and this is not a comforting thought (1 John 5:19). The open view grants this. Even God takes risks. But the world is less scary in this view than if we try to find consolation in the belief that everything that occurs is controlled by God and thus reflects his dubious character.

Appendix

Other Passages Supporting the Open View of God and the Future

In what follows, I will cite verses that suggest that the future is partly open and that God knows it as such. These are verses that were not discussed in chapter 2. I will offer a brief comment after each citation as to why I believe it is more compatible with the open view of God and the future than it is with the classical view of divine foreknowledge.

Numbers 11:1–2

The Lord was in the process of judging Israel by fire when Moses interceded in prayer "and the fire abated" (v. 2). A commonsense reading of the verse suggests that the fire would have continued had Moses not prayed. This suggests that God's plans are not eternally fixed, as the classical view of foreknowledge teaches.

Numbers 14:12–20

In response to Israel's bickering, the Lord says, "I will strike them with pestilence and disinherit them, and I will make of you [Moses] a nation greater and mightier than they" (v. 12). Moses asks the Lord to forgive the people, and the Lord eventually responds, "I do forgive, just as you have asked" (v. 20).

Unless the intention the Lord declared to Moses in verse 12 was insincere, we must conclude that he did not at that point intend to forgive the Israelites. It cannot have been certain at that time (let alone from all eternity) that God would forgive the Israelites. Hence, it seems that either the Lord is insincere, or the classical view of divine foreknowledge is mistaken.

Numbers 16:20–35

After Israel's sin under the leadership of Korah, the Lord said to Moses and Aaron, "Separate yourselves from this congregation, so that I may consume them in a moment" (v. 21). Moses and Aaron pleaded with the Lord to judge only those who were most guilty. In response, the Lord modified his judgment and gave the people a choice between himself or "wicked men" (v. 26).

The passage represents another instance of the Lord modifying his expressed intentions in response to prayer. If all of the future is exhaustively settled in God's mind, however, God's declared intention to "consume" the whole congregation could not have been sincere. He never really intended to do it, for he always foreknew he wouldn't do it. For all of the godly motives of those who defend the classical view of foreknowledge, it has the unfortunate consequence of depicting God as one who toys with us, using idle threats he has no intention of following through.

Numbers 16:41–48

The day following the Korah incident (see vv. 20–35), the Israelites rebelled against Moses again, this time because they blamed him for the death of those who were judged the day before (v. 41). The Lord was very angry because of this and said to Moses and Aaron, "Get away from this congregation, so that I may consume them in a moment" (v. 45). People immediately began to die from a plague (v. 46). Moses prayed while Aaron quickly "made atonement" for their sins, "and the plagued was stopped" (v. 48).

The view that the future is eternally settled in God's mind has the effect of undermining the honesty of God's expressed intention to judge Israel and the power of prayer to change God's mind as illustrated in this passage.

Judges 10:13–16

The Israelites cried out to God because of their oppression from foreign rulers. The Lord refused to deliver them because they had abandoned him (vv. 13–14). The Israelites repented, put away their foreign gods, and worshiped the Lord. The Lord "could no longer bear to see Israel suffer" (v. 16) and therefore changed his mind about the matter and fought once again on behalf of Israel.

If the whole of the future is eternally settled in the divine mind, God could not have been straightforward in declaring his intention *not* to deliver the Israelites from their plight—for he ended up doing just this. This passage, like so many others, shows God to be a relational God whose estimation of a relationship varies as the relationship varies. He is not locked into one course of action; as the God of possibilities, he is perfectly responsive to new circumstances that his free creations initiate.

1 Samuel 23:10–13

David heard that Saul knew that he was hiding in Keilah. Saul was seeking to kill David, so David wisely consulted the Lord as to what he should do.

> David said, "O LORD, the God of Israel, your servant has heard that Saul seeks to come to Keilah, to destroy the city on my account. And now, will Saul come down as your servant has heard? O LORD, the God of Israel, I beseech you, tell your servant." The LORD said, "He will come down." Then David said, "Will the men of Keilah surrender me and my men into the hand of Saul?" The LORD said, "They will surrender you." Then David and his men . . . set out and left Keilah.

This passage reveals that God's foreknowledge is not always about what *will* certainly happen; it is often about what *might* happen. The Lord tells David that Saul will come to Keilah and that the people of Keilah will deliver him over. David doesn't consider this a declaration of an unalterable future, however, for he immediately attempts to alter what the Lord just told him would happen! He leaves Keilah and thus avoids what God foretold would happen.

Biblical authors don't generally assume that God's declarations about the future are unalterable. Indeed, they sometimes chastise people for drawing just this conclusion (see Jer. 18:2–11). If the classical understanding of God's foreknowledge is correct, however, the future *is* unalterable! If God tells us what is coming in the future, it is no use to try to change it. The fact that the Word of God encourages us *not* to think this way suggests that the future is not exhaustively settled in reality, and thus not in the mind of God.

2 Samuel 24:12–16 (see also 1 Chronicles 21:7–13)

The Lord gives David three options of how Israel will be judged. "Three things I offer you; choose one of them, and I will do it to you" (v. 12). This verse reveals how the Lord gives people genuine alternatives and responds to their choices. If God foreknew what David would choose, however, the purpose of the offer is inexplicable.

2 Samuel 24:17–25

"So the LORD answered [David's] supplication for the land, and the plague was averted from Israel" (v. 25). The passage suggests that the Lord intended the plague to judge Israel further, but David's supplication persuaded him to change his mind. If the future is to some degree open and God is genuinely affected in the present by what we do and how we pray, the urgency that the Bible attaches to prayer begins to make sense. If everything is eternally settled, this urgency is compromised.

1 Kings 21:21–29

Because of Ahab's great sin the Lord tells him, "I will bring disaster on you; I will consume you" (v. 21). Ahab repents and the Lord responds by telling his messenger prophet, "Have you seen how Ahab has humbled himself before me?

Because he has humbled himself before me, I will not bring the disaster in his days" (v. 29).

The Lord revoked his prophecy against Ahab and delayed judging his descendants because of Ahab's repentance. If all of this was foreknown to God, his prophecy to Ahab that he was going to bring disaster and consume him could not have been given in earnest. If verse 21 expresses God's genuine intention, then we must conclude that God's mind can, indeed, change in the light of a shift in people's attitudes and actions (something the Lord explicitly tells us is true in other passages, e.g., Jer. 18:7–10).

2 Kings 13:3–5

The Lord judged the Israelites by allowing them to be oppressed by King Hazael of Aram (v. 3). "But Jehoahaz entreated the LORD, and the LORD *heeded him; for he saw* the oppression of Israel, how the king of Aram oppressed them. *Therefore* the LORD gave Israel a savior, so that they escaped from the hand of the Arameans" (vv. 4–5).

In the light of Jehoahaz's prayer and the severity of Hazael's oppressive treatment of Israel, God reversed his judgment. This verse, like many others, shows how God graciously alters his plans as a result of prayer and in the light of changing circumstances. Such flexibility makes sense only if the future is partly open and not exhaustively settled in God's mind.

2 Chronicles 7:12–14

The Lord says to Solomon, "When I shut up the heavens so that there is no rain, or command the locust to devour the land, or send pestilence among my people, if my people who are called by my name humble themselves, pray, seek my face, and turn from their wicked ways, then I will hear from heaven, and will forgive their sin and heal their land" (vv. 13–14).

This well-known verse describes the Lord's willingness to reverse judgment in the light of people's repentance (see also Jonah 4:2; Joel 2:13–14). When God judges his people by shutting up the heavens, he is willing to alter his course of action, relent from his punishment, and heal the people *if* they will pray, seek his face, and turn from their wicked ways. This is a picture of a God who is supremely responsive to the ever-changing circumstances of life in which free creatures are involved, not the picture of a God who eternally knows reality as a static block of unalterable facts.

Jeremiah 7:5–7

The Lord says to Israel, "*If* you truly amend your ways . . . *if* you truly act justly one with another, *if* you do not oppress the alien, the orphan, and the widow . . . and *if* you do not go after other gods . . . *then* I will dwell with you in this place."

The "if . . . then" clauses that the Lord uses throughout Scripture make the most sense if the future is to some extent a realm of possibilities. Suppose the Lord were to add the following to the conditional clauses found in this passage: "But of course I have known from all eternity that you will not amend your ways, act justly, refrain from oppressing aliens or chasing after idols, and thus I have been eternally certain that I will not dwell with you in this place." Would this not undermine the genuineness and force of the "if . . . then" clauses?

Jeremiah 38:17–18, 21

The Lord prophesies to Zedekiah, "*If* you will only surrender to the officials of the king of Babylon," the city and
his family would be spared, but "*if* you do not surrender,"
the city and his family would be destroyed. He then reiter-
ates, "But *if you are determined* not to surrender," even
Zedekiah himself would die.

The God of these verses states prophecies in conditional
terms, giving free moral agents the choice between alternatives. These choices seem meaningless if a particular outcome is exhaustively and eternally foreknown.

Ezekiel 20:5–22

The Lord recounts to Ezekiel how he "chose Israel" and
"swore to the offspring of the house of Jacob" that he would
be their God and deliver them from Egypt (vv. 5–6). But
even in Egypt, the Israelites wouldn't follow his ways. The
Lord then says, "Then I *thought* I would pour out my wrath
upon them and spend my anger against them in the midst
of the land of Egypt. But I acted for the sake of my name
. . . So I led them out of the land of Egypt" (vv. 8–10). Even
after this graciousness, they continued to rebel, however,
so the Lord adds, "Then I *thought* I would pour out my wrath
upon them in the wilderness, to make an end of them. But
I acted for the sake of my name" (vv. 13–14). [See also Exod.
32:11–14.] After continued rebellion, the Lord again
"*thought* [he] would pour out [his] wrath upon them and
send [his] anger against them . . . But [he] withheld [his]
hand . . ." (vv. 21–22).

If God is sincere in telling us he "thought" about carrying out the judgments he ultimately decided against, he
could not have foreknown with certainty he would *not* carry

out these deeds. The integrity of the Lord's self-disclosure in this passage depends on our willingness to accept that the Lord genuinely considered carrying out his judgment but then decided against it (see also Ps. 106:45; Hosea 11:8–9). We should also note that passages such as this in which the Lord tells us what he was thinking cannot be explained as describing things in terms of how they *appear* to us. There is nothing apparent about what the Lord is thinking; we only know what he thinks when he tells us.

Ezekiel 33:13–15

> When I say to the righteous he will surely live, and he so trusts in his righteousness that he commits iniquity, none of his righteous deeds will be remembered . . . he will die. But when I say to the wicked, "You shall surely die," and he turns from his sin and practices justice and righteousness, if a wicked man restores a pledge, pays back what he has taken by robbery, walks by the statutes which ensure life without committing iniquity, he will surely live; he shall not die (NASB).

How are we to understand the Lord telling a righteous person "you shall surely live" or telling a wicked person "you shall surely die" if we also believe that at that very moment the Lord was perfectly certain that the righteous person he is speaking to would not live (for he eternally foreknew they'd fall) and the wicked person he's speaking to would not die (for he eternally foreknew they'd repent)? Declarations are truthful only if they reflect sincere beliefs. But if God's knowledge about a person's fate is eternally settled, then any declaration he gives that goes against this knowledge seems insincere.

If we grant that when the Bible depicts God as changing his mind it depicts him as he truly is and not simply as he appears to us, these problems disappear. In good faith, the Lord tells the righteous they will live and the wicked they will die, for this is what the Lord truly believes about them at the time of the declaration. If the people change, however, his belief about them changes, and so his sincere declaration about them changes as well.

Hosea 11:8–9

After plotting severe judgment against Israel (vv. 5–7), the Lord says,

> My heart recoils within me;
>   my compassion grows warm and tender.
> I will not execute my fierce anger . . .
>   I will not come in wrath.

This passage shows that God experiences conflict between his compassion and his justice and that he sometimes alters his plans (his heart "recoils") as a result (see also 1 Chron. 21:11–15; Ezek. 20:5–22). He is a personal God who sometimes experiences conflicting emotions as he participates in the ups and downs of life with his people. Only a preconceived, philosophical ideal of what God is "supposed" to be like would ever suggest that this tender portrayal is evidence of weakness. In truth, God's responsiveness is a demonstration of his strength and wisdom.

Matthew 25:41

The Lord teaches that on the judgment day, he will say to the wicked, "Depart from me into the eternal fire *prepared for the devil and his angels*."

Hell was expressly prepared for "the devil and his angels"; humans were never meant to go there. But if God eternally knew that certain *people* would end up going to hell, one must wonder not only why this verse suggests that hell was prepared only for wicked angels but also why God created doomed individuals (or angels) at all.

Acts 15:7

At the Jerusalem council, "Peter stood up and said to them, 'My brothers, you know that in the early days God made a choice among you, that I should be the one through whom the Gentiles should hear the message of the good news.'"

This passage locates God's "choice" in "the early days," which strongly suggests that it wasn't made in the eternal past as the classical doctrine asserts. The God of the possible decides among possibilities as he moves along with us in time. After considering every variable, the Lord decided that choosing Peter to bring the Good News of Jesus Christ to the Gentiles best fit his sovereign purpose.

If everything is settled from all eternity in the mind of God, however, there is really nothing left to decide in time. Everything in Scripture as well as in our own experience suggesting that God makes decisions or reverses previous decisions as he moves with us into the future must be mistaken.

Acts 21:10–12

While Paul and Luke were making preparations to go and preach in Jerusalem, "a prophet named Agabus came down from Judea" (v. 10). The prophet approached Paul,

168

took his belt, and announced, "Thus says the Holy Spirit, 'This is the way the Jews in Jerusalem will bind the man who owns this belt and will hand him over to the Gentiles'" (v. 11). Luke then records that when Paul's comrades heard this, they "urged him not to go up to Jerusalem" (v. 12).

Several things are interesting about Agabus's prophecy. First, it is clear from the response of Paul's comrades that they did not consider this prophetic message to be a declaration of what was certainly going to happen in the future, for they immediately tried to persuade Paul *not* to go to Jerusalem (v. 12). Instead, they interpreted the prophecy as a warning about what would happen to Paul *if* he chose to go to Jerusalem. They assume that whether this would come to pass or not was for Paul to decide.

Second, it is interesting to note that even after Paul decided to go to Jerusalem, things did not transpire exactly as Agabus had prophesied. When Paul was discovered by some of his fellow Jews in the temple, a riot broke out and he was beaten by the crowd (vv. 27–30). They were about to kill him (v. 31) when Roman guards arrived on the scene, arrested him, and thereby saved him from the hostile mob (vv. 32–33). Contrary to Agabus's prophecy, the Jews never bound Paul and handed him over to the Romans. Instead, the Romans rescued Paul from the Jews.

Such a turn of events is troubling to the classical understanding of divine foreknowledge and the understanding of divine prophecy that usually accompanies it. If God knows every detail about the future activity of free agents, there's no explanation for the fact that things did not happen exactly as the Holy Spirit had prophesied through Agabus.

If the future is partly composed of possibilities and probabilities, however, then this prophecy is a perfect assessment of what would *generally* happen based on the Lord's perfect knowledge of the present disposition of the Jews in

Jerusalem. The Jews were going to be hostile toward Paul, and, given the political structure of the time, he would eventually end up in the hands of the Romans. But precisely because a myriad of free agents were involved, there was an element of openness in exactly how things were played out.

At the time of Agabus's prophecy, it was most probable that the Jews would seize Paul and hand him over to the Romans. The Holy Spirit, who knows all things perfectly, accurately reported this. As it turned out, however, the situation had worsened since the time of the prophecy, and consequently, Paul was nearly killed.

Though we can't be certain of this, God's providential hand may be discerned in the speed with which the riot was reported to the Romans and the speed with which the Romans dispatched a unit to break it up. If God's sovereign purposes for history required Paul's ministry to continue, God would certainly influence matters in creative ways as much as he needed to in order to prevent Paul's untimely death. In other words, there's no reason to conclude that it was simply good luck that saved Paul's life and thus allowed him to become a foundational pillar and author in the New Testament church. But neither is there any reason to conclude that everything surrounding this episode was preplanned or foreknown by God.

In his wisdom and power, the "God of the possible" is prepared for and capable of responding to every contingency, however improbable, that might arise. He can ingeniously achieve his sovereign purposes while still allowing for a significant element of free will (see also Exod. 3:18–4:9).

Notes

Introduction

1. All scriptural citations are from the NRSV. All italicization of Scripture passages are added by the author.

2. There is, of course, a sense in which *all* talk about God is nonliteral. When we say God "thinks," "loves," or "acts justly," for example, we are saying that God engages in activities that are analogous to what we do when we think, love, or act justly. Given this proviso, however, it still is meaningful to insist that God literally "thinks," "loves," or "acts justly" and mean by this that these statements describe God *as he truly is*. This view would contrast with a view that might hold that God doesn't *really* "think," "love," or "act justly"; it just *looks* that way from our limited perspectives. My only point is that the language about God "changing his mind," "regretting," and so on should be taken no less literally than language about God "thinking," "loving," or "acting justly."

3. The phrase "as the future is now" may sound paradoxical because it may seem that "the future" is by definition what is later, not now. Actually, the meaning of the phrase is not paradoxical. Ordinarily, we have two distinct ways of thinking and speaking about the future. The future is sometimes spoken of as what *will* occur, other times as what *may* occur. If one is speaking in the former sense, it is meaningless to speak of the future "as the future is now." In the second mode of speech, however, it makes perfect sense to speak of the future "as the future is now," for what the future is now (what *may* occur) is different from what the future *will* be when it becomes the present (what actually comes to pass).

4. I will develop this thesis in detail in a forthcoming book entitled *The Myth of the Blueprint* (Downers Grove, Ill.: InterVarsity, forthcoming).

Chapter 1: The Classical View of Divine Foreknowledge

1. Among other things, process theology holds that God needs the world. He could not have existed without it. It also denies the omnipotence of God. For an evangelical critique of process theology, see R. Nash, ed., *Process Theology* (Grand Rapids: Baker, 1987).

2. Many times God speaks in terms that *seem* unconditional, though a condition is implied. He told Jonah that he was going to destroy Nineveh in forty days (3:4), only to "change his mind" when they repented (3:10). Clearly, God's announcement of destruction

was *not* unconditional. See Jeremiah 18:7–10, where the Lord reserves the right to "change his mind" whenever he sees fit. In this light, we must concede that the Lord's prophecy about the coming four hundred years of slavery might have been conditional. Perhaps it did not *have* to take place.

3. As some exegetes argue, it is possible to interpret Jesus' prediction to Peter as a conditional prophecy. Jesus was warning Peter, hoping he wouldn't deny him. In my estimation, this interpretation is less likely than the one I offer here.

4. The opposite side of this truth may be found in Acts 13:48, where Luke summarizes the Gentiles' response to Paul's preaching by saying that, "as many as had been *destined for* eternal life became believers." The text does not say that these people were destined for eternal life *from the beginning of time.* This would contradict the scriptural teaching that God does not arbitrarily select who will and will not be saved (Ezek. 18:23, 32; 33:11; 1 Tim. 2:4; 4:10; 2 Peter 3:9; 1 John 2:2). Rather, the text simply implies that by the time the Gentiles heard the gospel, some had already had their hearts opened up to God by the Holy Spirit and thus were "destined" to believe and be saved (see Acts 16:14). We will discuss the relationship between the work of the Holy Spirit and the free will of people in chapter 4, question 12.

5. Though it would take us too far astray to discuss the matter, many Bible scholars maintain that at least some messianic prophecies are *illustrative, not predictive.* In this view, New Testament authors cite certain Old Testament passages to note that Jesus' life and death *illustrate* what the passages are about, not to show that Jesus' life *had* to unfold in a particular manner. If this view is accepted, one could argue that no one *had* to betray Jesus. But given the fact that by the time of the Last Supper it was certain Judas was going to betray Jesus, David's betrayal by a close friend a thousand years earlier (Ps. 41:9) could now be cited as an inspired anticipation of what Jesus was going to go through. Declaring his knowledge of this inspired pattern would help demonstrate Jesus' divinity and strengthen the faith of the disciples.

6. It may be that when Scripture declares that God sent forth his Son at the right time, it is saying that the conditions were ideal for God to achieve his purposes (Rom. 5:6; Mark 1:15; Gal. 4:4).

7. The view that Revelation is primarily about events prior to A.D. 70 is called the "preterist" interpretation of Revelation (though some preterists hold that it refers to events at the end of the first century). The view that Revelation is primarily about providing readers with a symbolic pattern of God's conflict with Satan throughout history is called the "idealist" interpretation. I suggest that it is possible to affirm both views as essentially correct. For an overview of these two views as well as two other possible interpretations of the Book of Revelation, including the "futuristic" view, see C. Marvin Pate, ed., *Four Views on the Book of Revelation* (Grand Rapids: Zondervan, 1998).

Chapter 3: What Practical Difference Does the Open View Make?

1. See G. Boyd and E. Boyd, *Letters from a Skeptic* (Wheaton: Victor, 1992), 29–31.

2. For a fuller treatment of the problem of evil from this perspective, see Gregory Boyd, *Satan and the Problem of Evil: Constructing a Warfare Theodicy* (Downers Grove, Ill.: InterVarsity, forthcoming).

3. See G. Boyd, *God at War: The Bible and Spiritual Conflict* (Downers Grove, Ill.: InterVarsity, 1996), 169–269.

4. See P. Coveney and R. Highfield, *The Arrow of Time* (New York: Fawcett Columbine, 1990).

Chapter 4: Questions and Objections

1. See Gerard Verbeke, *The Presence of Stoicism in Medieval Thought* (Washington, D.C.: Catholic University Press of America, 1983), 82–83. See also J. Den Boeft, *Calcidius on Fate: His Doctrine and Sources* (New York: Brill, 1997); J. H. Waszink, ed., *Timaeus a Calcidio translatus Commentarioque instructus*, 2d ed., Plato Latinus, vol. 4 (Leiden: Brill, 1975).

2. See L. D. McCabe, *Divine Nescience of Future Contingencies a Necessity* (New York: Philips & Hunt, 1882); idem, *The Foreknowledge of God* (Cincinnati: Cranston & Stowe, 1887); B. Hibbard, *Memoirs of the Life and Travels of B. Hibbard*, 2d ed. (New York: Piercy & Reed, 1843), 372–414. It is worth noting that though this view was debated at this time, no one was pronounced "heretical" for holding it.

3. Commenting on the African-American view of God, Major Jones writes: "We [in the African Christian tradition] believe human actions to be truly free, such that whereas God's knowledge of the past is total and absolute, God's knowledge of future events is not yet complete, particularly so far as acts of human freedom are concerned. The perfection of divine omniscience, then, must be construed to be God's always perfectly increasing knowledge taking in, with the passage of time, all knowable reality as it expands. Not to know as real and sure what is, as yet, neither sure nor real is not imperfection; to know the unreal and the unsure as uncertain and still forming is to know perfectly whatever is to be known" (*The Color of God: The Concept of God in Afro-American Thought* [Macon, Ga.: Mercer Press, 1987], 95). Jones forcefully argues that the African-American experience of oppression has enabled them to seize a dimension of the biblical portrait of God (including the openness of God) that the classical Western tradition missed because of its infatuation with control and its indebtedness to Platonic philosophy. I find myself in substantial agreement with this analysis.

4. It could be argued that the "middle knowledge" understanding of divine foreknowledge ascribes to God the same infinitely vast amount of knowledge as does the open view. This view holds that God not only knows what *will* be but what *would have been* under every possible different set of circumstances. Even if the point is conceded, the view still has an inferior concept of God's wisdom, for it regards both the actual world that God will be and every possible world that God knows might have been as settled ahead of time. Hence, God doesn't genuinely have to *anticipate possibilities* in this view, for he eternally knows which possibilities will and will not be actualized.

5. Plato, *Timaeus*, trans. Benjamin Jowett, in *Plato: The Collected Dialogues*, ed. Edith Hamilton and Huntington Cairns (Princeton: Princeton University Press, 1961), 1167.

6. In a forthcoming volume, I demonstrate historically that most of the responsibility for the canonization of the "timeless" model of perfection in the Christian theological tradition rests on St. Augustine. He was in this respect strongly influenced not only by Platonism but by Stoicism and Manichaeism as well. See G. Boyd, *The Myth of the Blueprint* (Downers Grove, Ill.: InterVarsity Press, forthcoming).

7. See also Deuteronomy 10:17–19; 2 Chronicles 19:7; Job 34:19; Isaiah 55:4–5; Ezekiel 18:25; Mark 12:14; John 3:16; Romans 2:10–11; Ephesians 6:9; 1 Peter 1:17.

8. A defender of exhaustive foreknowledge who held to "middle knowledge" (see note 4, above) could argue that God foreknew the possibility of you getting robbed and warned you on the basis of this knowledge, but he *also* foreknew with certainty that you would or would not heed this warning. Whatever else may be said about this view, it does not give the believer any more security than the open view. Our trust in God's ability to change things is associated with his foreknowledge of possibilities that *can* be altered, not certainty of what *cannot* be altered.

Scripture Index

Genesis

3 64
3:8–9 59
6:3 38
6:5–6 105
6:6 55
15:13–14 26
15:13–15 33
22:12 64

Exodus

3:18 67
3:18–4:9 169
4:1 67
4:5 67
4:8 67
4:9 67
4:10–15 62
4:14 62
13:17 69
16:4 65
32:11–14 164
32:14 63, 83
32:33 42, 74
33:1–3 83
33:14 83

Numbers

11:1–2 63, 157
11:2 157
14:11 58–59
14:12 158
14:12–20 63, 158
14:20 158
16:20–35 63, 158, 159

16:21 158
16:26 158
16:41 159
16:41–48 63, 159
16:45 159
16:46 159
16:48 159
22:38–23:17 80
23:19 79, 80, 136

Deuteronomy

4:34 118
8:2 65
9:13–14 63
9:13–29 83
9:18–20 63
9:20 83
9:25 63, 83
9:25–29 83
10:17–19 172 n. 7
13:1–3 65
30:19 138

Judges

2:22 65
3:4 65
10:13–14 159
10:13–16 63, 159
10:16 159

1 Samuel

2:27–31 83
2:30–31 83
13:13 56
13:13–14 79
15:10 56

15:11 79, 86, 105
15:11–12 80
15:27 80
15:29 79, 80
15:35 56, 79, 105
23:10–13 160

2 Samuel

24:12 161
24:12–16 161
24:17–25 63, 161
24:25 161

1 Kings

13:2–3 26
21:21 83, 161, 162
21:21–29 63, 83, 161
21:29 84, 161–162
22:20 59

2 Kings

13:3 162
13:3–5 63, 162
13:4–5 162
20 8
20:1 7
20:1–6 63, 82
20:6 7, 82, 123
22:1 26
23:15–16 26

1 Chronicles

21:7–13 161
21:11–15 166
21:15 81

2 Chronicles

7:12–14 162
7:13–14 162–163
7:14 97
12:5 84
12:5–8 63, 84
12:7 84
19:7 172 n. 7
32:31 64

Job

34:19 172 n. 7

Psalms

17:8 118
41:9 171 n. 5
95:10–11 66
106:23 83
106:45 165
139 41
139:16 26, 39, 40, 41

Proverbs

16:4 38

Isaiah

5:1–7 119
5:2 59
5:4 59
5:5 59
38:1–5 42
44:28 26
46 29
46:9–10 25, 30
46:10 30

173

4:7 155
4:15 37

2 Thessalonians

2:3–4 28–29, 49

1 Timothy

2:3–4 100
2:4 46, 138, 140,
  171 n. 4
4:1 28
4:1–3 49
4:3 28
4:10 138, 171 n. 4

2 Timothy

1:9 28, 47

Hebrews

1:2 49
1:3 69
3:7–10 66
3:8 66, 73, 138
3:15 73, 138
4:7 73, 138
6:18 60, 136

James

1:13 136
1:17 136

1 Peter

1:17 172 n. 7
1:20 27, 45, 49

2 Peter

3:7–10 49
3:9 11, 40, 46–47,
  58, 71, 73, 100,
  138, 140,
  171 n. 4
3:9–12 72
3:12 71

1 John

2:2 138, 171 n. 4
5:19 156
1:1 50
1:3 50
1:4 50
2:16 50
3:5 42, 74

3:10–11 50
13:5 50
13:8 45
13:18 50
22:6 50
22:7 50
22:10 50
22:12 50
22:18 74
22:19 74
22:20 50

Gregory A. Boyd (Ph.D., Princeton Theological Seminary) is professor of theology at Bethel College, where he has taught since 1986. He is also senior pastor of Woodland Hills Church (Baptist General Conference), a megachurch located in St. Paul, Minnesota. He is the author of seven books, including *Letters from a Skeptic,* an ECPA Gold Medallion Award winner; *Cynic Sage or Son of God,* a *Christianity Today* Book Award winner; and *God at War.*